DENIAL

DENIAL

MY TWENTY-FIVE YEARS WITHOUT A SOUL

Jonathan Rauch

Acorn Abbey

Copyright © 2013, 2019 Jonathan Rauch

Published 2019 by Acorn Abbey Books
Madison, North Carolina
All rights reserved

Second edition
with a new afterword
by the Author

ISBN 978-1-949450-01-9

First published April 2013, The Atlantic Books

**Acorn Abbey Books
Madison, North Carolina
acornabbey.com**

PRCS0120190801

Cover design by Dan Smith

For Michael,
my husband,
who closed this chapter

1

I HAVE a peculiar memory which must date to when I was ten or eleven years old. I am sitting at the piano daydreaming one afternoon, and it occurs to me that I will never get married. Simultaneously with this realization comes the recognition that I have always understood that marriage was unlikely for me, and that today is merely the first time I have said so, to myself, "aloud." So baldly clear is this realization that I might as well be acknowledging that I will never have eight legs and spin a web. Even so, the revelation strikes me as peculiar. Almost all the adults I know are married, and so, for that matter, are most of the grown-ups I have ever heard of. Everyone gets married. Why, then, do I know that the world of married adults has no connection to me, and that I will go off in some different direction? The strange thing about this moment, both when it occurs and later on in retrospect—perhaps the reason I recall it at all—is the otherworldly blandness of a realization which is as certain as it is apparently baseless. Marriage is not relevant to me, and that is a fact. And then I shrug and pass on to other thoughts, all of them lost to me now.

I recall childhood as a series of moments in a continual present thrust right up in my face, with no past or future. Though I learned, I do not remember acquiring knowledge. My discovery on that afternoon came as an announcement which presented itself with a bow and sat down to take its appointed place in my conscious mind. It must have been, however, part of a long unfolding. A few things had gone before, and later would come many others. Only in retrospect was I able to find any pattern in the skein. And what a strange pattern it turned out to be! To have been twisted up in it, controlled by it, bent and helpless like a tied tree! Today, as I look back from middle age, the contorted condition of my youth has become incomprehensible to me. What you read here is a piecing together of shards, a backwards reading of an ancient script. The feeling which made sense of that world is gone, thank God.

I want to say, with my eyes dry and my throat unlumped, that I have no special claim on anyone's sympathy. Perhaps just the opposite. Strangeness and misperception are constitutive elements of childhood and young adulthood. It is probably a contradiction in terms to speak of an "ordinary" childhood. The whole period has aspects of a visionary insanity: the obsessive fascination with certain random objects, each of which has not only qualities but its own personality (to children, things are people and people are things, as Walt Disney understood); the vast yet incoherent quality of space and time, which roll on and on yet never flow into a whole; the bellowing caprice and excruciating boringness of grown-ups, who are useful but never interesting. Those years are a farrago of explosive joys and horrors, and although everyone cherishes their magic, only a fool wishes they lasted any longer. Compared with children who were abused or ostracized or neglected or impoverished, I was lucky. My peculiar deformity was far from the worst problem which a child or a man (it lasted well into adulthood) can have.

I do maintain, however, that it was easily among the most *perplexing* of the distortions which can give youth its outlandish peculiarity. There is no possible preparation for it and no visible exit from it. To the extent one hears it discussed at all, it is as a problem of "homosexual youth," or "the closet." But to speak that way, although adequate from a school counselor's or gay activist's point of view, is to misconceive the whole case. Homosexuality is a fact, albeit a fact with many implications. What I experienced was not a fact at all, and certainly not a sexual fact. Rather, it was an elaborate structure of interwoven denials which grew around and then over the fact of sexuality, a kudzu which first covered and then obliterated the foliage beneath. Sexuality of any sort became impossible; so did love. The bland vanilla certainty that marriage was impossible for me brought with it a further, not-bland certainty, that love too was impossible. It was simply not provided for in my constitution. Every day I could feel, if I stopped to notice, that some essential capacity was missing, although most days, until I was in my teens, I did not care very much. Then I cared a lot. The world was bursting in all around me and my mind was staggering to keep up, and, as though all of that was not enough, I had been born without a soul. What is a self, after all, but a soul, and what is a soul without love and without even the capacity for love? The soul is a sovereign, but without love it has no kingdom. In a matter-of-fact way, I began to understand that I was a monster.

A word I think of in this connection is an old bit of psychiatric jargon which went out of polite use a few decades ago. Today the word *invert* is scarcely ever heard at all. Not so long ago, however, it was not only reputable but clinically descriptive. In those days, homosexuality was often regarded not merely as a sexual disorder or perversion, like impotence or exhibitionism, but as a comprehensive personality disorder. That is, homosexuality was not just a thing unto itself: it was a marker of a disturbed and possibly antisocial or even dangerous character. The invert's sexuality was an expression of a deep tangle of neuroses. He was thus quite a sick person, unfit for military service or positions of social responsibility. Socially, the invert was likely to be backward and poorly adjusted; psychologically, he was not only unhappy but the very antithesis of normalcy. Thus was his personality almost literally upside-down. Now, the dusty museum case is a good resting place for *invert*, and I would hate to see it creep back into general use. But I cannot deny that in some respects, it is a good word to describe what I was for 25 years.

An analogy which I sometimes find helpful is that of a photographic negative. Things—events, people, feelings—are in proper proportion and relation to each other. Nothing is visibly "wrong," nothing unintelligible. B follows from A and black shades properly into white. You could manage to live this way for a long time, perhaps for a whole lifetime, and make out all right. You would not be unhappier than it is many people's lot in life to be. But then one fine day, a light shines through the negative and its image is cast onto photographic paper and a positive is produced. And then the past and the entirety of one's self, once so sensible and self-contained, are seen to have been ludicrous, a backwards reading of reality which had allowed every detail to be seen yet not a single one to register as it should have. All, then, is revealed to have been an inversion; and I, in an exquisitely apt sense, an invert.

My inversion ended many years ago. Every day it recedes

further into dream. Recalling the texture and warp of the looking-glass world, I feel like the man whose migraines are long cured but who seeks to recall and record the visions he saw when he was afflicted. I do not claim that my experience was typical, or that a quite "typical" homosexual childhood, or a "typical" heterosexual childhood, actually exists. I do not claim anything, except that other youths experience something at least similar to what happened to me, and that describing what happened may therefore be interesting. A metallurgist learns the properties of a new alloy by twisting and bending and melting and otherwise deforming it. A cognitive psychologist learns how vision works by tricking it with illusions. Might one not learn something about the nature of the loving soul by considering the case of a person who grew up without one?

2

EVEN IN my earliest years, I was deeply fascinated by outward symbols of masculinity. I was five or so—this was still in the little house on Fourteenth Street, before we moved to a more posh part of Phoenix—when I became aware that a cartoon character called Sinbad Jr. obsessed me in a way I could not begin to define. He was a young man or boy with a magic belt. When he was in trouble, he yanked on the belt and his chest swelled and his arms bulged and he became a hero of superhuman strength, equal to any challenge. I conceived an intense desire to own a Sinbad Jr. belt. I schemed and plotted to get one, imagining feverishly where I might buy one. Yes, of course, Sinbad Jr. was only an animated cartoon, and even a preschooler knows the difference between a cartoon and reality. Still, I was not quite sure where the border lay between reality and magic, and I knew that a local children's TV show offered Sinbad Jr.

belts as prizes. With such a prize, I could play at being Sinbad Jr., or (who could tell?) I could actually *be* Sinbad Jr. I wonder if I asked my parents for a Sinbad Jr. belt. I think I probably did. If so, that would have been unusual. Perhaps the single most harrowing feature of my inversion was the dark secrecy in which it shrouded me: along with the Sinbad Jr. fascination, and all the other fascinations that followed it, came an understanding that the obsession was not normal and must be hidden at all costs. Without being told, I knew it was weird. It *seemed* weird. In fact, of course, there is nothing particularly strange in a little boy's adulation for a cartoon character, or in his desire for a magic belt to make him big and strong. No playtime fantasy could have been more boyishly banal. But my version of this fantasy was freighted with a strange power. This was more than playing Batman and punching invisible enemies in the stomach. I wanted in a deeper, more slavishly yearning way to *be* Sinbad Jr., to feel myself wrapped in him, to fasten his belt around my boyish waist and feel hard muscle—his or mine or what, really, was the difference?

But what was wrong even with that? No one had told me, at that sheltered age, of homosexuality or sodomy or fairies or poofs. The very idea of sexuality, my own or anybody else's, would not present itself for years. Perhaps, then, I absorbed the knowledge of my abnormality by means of that magical osmosis through which children absorb the world? No doubt. But homophobic cultural tropes and media stereotypes and all the rest do not, it seems to me, fully explain why a kindergartner would classify his Sinbad Jr. fascination top secret, as instinctively as a cat buries its turds. No: from the age when they are old enough to comprehend a cartoon, children have some sense of what is normal, and they understand that not to be normal is a very serious crime. Little boys and teenagers want many things, but most of all they want to be normal. The desire not to be strange is not, I think, the callous invention of a capitalist or Protestant or racist or sexist or whateverist culture which seeks to repress human beings' explosively variegated diversity. It is, for people, an indivisible part of the socializing instinct. That is why children are so easily embarrassed by their parents. The instinct which teaches children how not to be little sociopaths also instructs them, unremittingly, to conform. I have heard, secondhand, of a few gay people who even as little children made no effort to hide their differentness: who, say, joyfully cross-dressed without a thought of secrecy. I think such people, if they in fact exist, will always be as rare as black pearls. In any case, I was not one of them. Even in the Sinbad Jr. days, I had begun to suspect the truth: something inside me was tugging very hard and was abnormal, and I was the only person in the world, the only person maybe ever, who was like this, and there was some fierce danger in letting on or giving in.

One night I was riding with some other boys in the

back of Mrs. Marshall's station wagon, sitting cross-legged. We passed beneath streetlights, and every few seconds the light flashed through the back of the car and illuminated Lee Lafontaine's blond hair. He was a medium-size boy, bigger and taller and more robustly built than I, with sun-browned skin and what seemed then a gravelly voice (I wonder now how a boy can have one) and the quality of easy leadership which makes some boys radiant, aristocrats among their classmates. The flashes of light made his hair glow silver and, just where the blond hair was etched against darkness, gave him a platinum halo. I realized I was staring. I could not take my eyes off his face and his hair. They were thrilling, fascinating, though I could not imagine why. I was carrying a small plastic pocket comb. Here, I said to Lee, this is a great comb, it feels great and it makes your hair incredibly shiny. I gave it to him and he stroked his hair and I imagined, as I watched, that I was Lee and smiling radiantly as I felt my brown hand slip through my blond hair, and I, too, was perfect. When he handed the comb back to me, it tingled, for there was some Lee on it. Ordinarily, at that age (seven or eight, by then), I treated other people's combs and drinking glasses and toothbrushes as though they carried leprosy, but from a comb touched by Lee, I might get something good. I might get Leeness. Again came a feeling, which became frequent, of wanting to creep inside him and then swell up, until I filled the whole space of his body and luxuriated in it.

DENIAL

By this time, I had passed well into reading age. People say that one of the most important of all engines in advancing literacy and communications technology, from movable type straight down to the internet, has been the male hunger for erotica. I believe it. I soon learned that words and images had mysterious powers, often as unpredictable and individual as flesh-and-blood people. My father disapproved of comic books, but occasionally let me have one or two. I approached this treat with a hidden agenda. At the comic-book rack, I would pull down one after another, inspecting each with a quick expert eye to appraise the power—over me—of its superhero. Batman was somehow too tough, Spiderman too thin; I cast them aside. But Superman had some superpowers. I never much liked him, either as a character or as a series. He was bland and too much the cast-iron juggernaut to be interesting, whereas Daredevil lived by his wits. Oh, but he had something else: flowing, rippling muscles, exposed by his painted-on "costume." Look how his arms bulge and his calves flair. Look, above all, at the Superchest: hard and barrel-thick. There was one episode I read again and again, kneading and fantasizing my way to a shivery twitch between the legs. Superman is tricked into donning doctored goggles and uses his X-ray vision, which backfires and paralyzes him. Then into a fiendish chair he is strapped, side by side with his nemesis, who, like me, is greedy for strength. Throw the switch, and the contraption begins transferring Superman's strength into his rival's body. "My muscles," exclaims the villain, first in exhilaration, then in agony, "my sinews! They're expanding like balloons!" Here was indeed a fantastic idea: *my* muscles and sinews, hardening and swelling and engorged with newfound power! I was like Sinbad Jr., except this time, instead of inchoate fascination, there was a very particular physical thrill.

It was strength which I worshipped, strength I adored. Everywhere, all the time, in books and at school and peering out of car windows as city blocks rolled by, I searched left to right lest I miss its outward sign, the muscular male physique. Every rolled-up sleeve presented possibilities, and none passed without undergoing inspection. Every so often, I would be rewarded with a little tidal wave which knocked me over and sent me spinning underwater. When I was nine, a summer-camp junior counselor named Ian, a thin young man I had paid little attention to, lifted me from the back of a pickup truck and set me down on the ground, effortlessly. There was that tingling convulsion again. To have been, literally, manhandled by Ian set my pulse racing. When I remarked, as innocuously as I could, that that had seemed pretty easy for him, he must be pretty strong, he pulled up his sleeve to bend what I had taken to be a mundanely ordinary arm, and I boggled at the rocky bulge. He let me touch it! And it burned my palm. From then on I kept an eye on Ian day and night, "collecting" any further examples of his strength. When he boasted to some campers of pulling apart a pair of stuck elevator doors with his bare hands—like *this*, hands locked together as arms struggled to pull them apart—I could think of little else for days. He had no idea that he had just then jolted me with a thousand volts of current. By that time, the effect such things had on me was unambiguously hydraulic. Plainly, whatever virus I had come down with was more than an interest in stamps or bugs or baseball. It was now something which was capable of roaring through me like a flash flood. Of course, I never mentioned it to a soul, and took pains to betray no unusual interest in Ian or his strength. I saw no parallel for my obsession. In camp, boys traded ghost stories and dirty jokes in the bunks late at night with not a hint of interest in Ian, and at school the boys went about their business oblivious to the omnipresent smell of muscle and masculinity which at any moment could overwhelm me like a waft of chlorine gas. Whatever signals I was receiving were transmitted to nobody else. Better, then, to hush and ignore. In time, I knew, I would grow up and then this strange business would pass. Better to wait it out.

In elementary school, I was bullied a bit, though never severely. If I was never beaten up, that was partly because I was willing to be humiliated. I was besotted with strong, athletic boys, and so it was my role to kneel before them. They were strong, I was weak. It was only natural that I should adore them. Adore them I did, though it was more like a combination of hero-worship and bitter frustration, in those pre-adolescent years, than anything which could properly be regarded as infatuation.

In the fifth grade, I realized that boys' and men's hands could look powerful and competent, or smoothly fat or weakly thin. I discovered myself savoring boys' hands with my eyes, gazing at wrist and thumb and palm as though hoping to burn every detail into my retinas. I noticed stomachs and legs and arms. I kept an eye on the phys-ed instructor, in case his short-sleeved shirt crept above the elbow and revealed a glimpse of strong arm. I marveled when my friend Nathan threw a stone, easily, half again as far as I could. Sitting next to him on the school bus, I let my eyes glide admiringly over the contours of his hand or slide along the steep slope of his shoulder.

All such glimpses of male perfection I collected and filed, but they were not enough. I was a human radar dish, tuned to sweep every frequency, day and night, for sightings of muscular masculinity. These days, muscular male models advertise everything everywhere. Buses chug around bearing ads in which a shirtless muscle god holds, irrelevantly, a Samsung microwave oven. In my boyhood, male models were safely avuncular and, of course, clothed. Nothing there for me. So I scoured the backs of comic books for ads showing bulging biceps or washboard stomachs. I read and reread the Charles Atlas ad in which the skinny runt returns in an armor of new muscles and sends the beach bully packing ("Hero of the Beach!").

In the bookstore near my father's office downtown, I never failed, after having ransacked the science-fiction shelf, to do investigative work in the sports department. Once in a while my luck would look up and I would find a book with some muscles in it. When that happened, it was like water for the parched, and I would simply stand in the bookstore drinking it up. I was especially keen on one small paperback, a beginner's guide to bodybuilding, with photos that made my heart batter the walls of my chest. One picture showed a swarthy man bathed in oil which made his muscles glisten in clenched ecstasy. He was a 1960s bodybuilder by the name of Harold Poole. Much later, as an adult, I saw that photo of him again, and was surprised by how much my imagination had magnified his physique. As a boy, however, I was overcome. At night, I would imagine coming across this man walking toward me in an alley or on a dead-end street at night. He would be wearing a white, loose-fitting shirt, which would just hint at the mountains of power and the shiny dark skin below; and then, for me—for me!—he would open the shirt and let it slip away and there would be those glistening muscles. Except now (somehow) they were mine, and I could feel the hardness of biceps against forearm as I cocked an elbow which was mine or his or ours. I thought about him often—and did more than think, as a boy of that age will.

As time went on, I accumulated a stack of muscle magazines, which I kept in a cabinet next to my bed. By night, by day, whenever, I would open one and find a picture of an overwhelmingly muscular man and look very hard at him. If I looked hard enough, which was easy to do, he would stir into motion. He would ever so slowly draw his fingers into a fist and then draw the fist inward toward the elbow and squeeze until the forearm was a veiny explosion of sinew, and then he bent his elbow until the biceps balled up and jammed against the iron forearm, and then, not finished yet, he let his arms fall to his sides and then stretched them out and up and behind his head and drew breath into his chest until it nearly burst, and he looked at me like a lion flashing his mane, daring me to imagine that any man so strong and indomitable might exist. Then, if I looked even harder, I could see myself approach him there in my room, just near the bed, and he would let me try to encircle his arm with my hands, but it was no use, his arm was too big to encompass, the best I could do was cup my hand over the biceps and feel how it pushed right through my palm, the hardness an eruption of marble. And then he would seize me and lift me, and for him this was as easy as lifting a feather pillow, those piston arms as inexorable as a forklift. Up, up I went, helpless in his hands, spinning, spinning in their grasp, gasping at his strength, until I gained release. And then at last I would put him away.

DENIAL

The terrible problem was what to tell myself about all this. Always, I emphasize, there was a *physical* sensation associated with these sightings. It was a tingling or a burning like frustration, or an excitement like fear. And of course, before I got very old, there was more than sensation, there was arousal. What—what in the world—was that? What did I think I was doing? What could it possibly all lead to? In what conceivable universe might this be a sensible way for a human being to feel or behave? If I had collected detailed appraisals of girls' hands or breasts, that might have seemed comprehensible. But this? Dismally I reflected, ruminating on the problem like a little goat.

Some homosexual boys are lucky enough to know, from an early age, that they wish to touch another boy sexually. Those boys, even if they are troubled by their desires, at least have something to go on. Their feelings, however unconventional or wrong, point to some plan of action. Mine left me mystified. At no time did I feel—or, maybe, did I allow myself to feel—the desire to *do* anything with another boy. If some preternaturally perceptive adult had pierced my intense secrecy and guessed all of my outlandish obsessions, and had sat me down to explain that my feelings were sexual or presexual, I simply would not have believed it. Sex, I knew even then, had something to do with other people's genitals and with certain obscure and acrobatic types of activity. It did not mean feeling a jolt when I noticed the veins in a man's forearm.

I was a bright, rational boy. I needed to understand my obsession as at least possibly sensible. It could not be—did not feel remotely like—mere random weirdness. I needed an explanation. And so I invented one. Or, rather, many. And those, rather than the feelings they were constructed around, were what made me inverted, far beyond just being homosexual or even pre-homosexual. I developed a theory, as it were, of love and sexuality which turned love into envy and sexual feeling into self-loathing. I turned the world upside-down.

3

WHAT I WANT to talk about now may embarrass you. It embarrasses me. It is not prurient or kinky, particularly, but it is ridiculous in the infantile way of any immature love or obsession. Mozart and Jane Austen look pretty good when judged by their tastes and works at age fourteen, but for most of us, revisiting a childish obsession is like rereading a seventh-grade book report. I do not think I could have done much differently than I did, even with the sort of adult guidance which would have been unthinkable for me to seek. (What if they pack me off to the funny farm? What could they tell me that could possibly not be bad news?) But dear God, what a botch I made of it.

My thinking for a long time was as follows: I was just a little boy: a child. I had a kind of kink in me which made no sense whatever, but this was all right. The reason it was all right was that it would go away. It was only natural for me, a small, unathletic child, to feel a kind of burning admiration for physically commanding boys and to yearn for big biceps. And, obviously, this would account for the odd behavior which I seemed impelled toward, and for the peculiar tingling. I was literally tingling with envy. Not to worry, however, for I was a well-informed boy, and I knew what would soon come to pass. I would reach a certain magical age and two magical things would happen. First, I would grow up and my body would swell with masculine heft and I would look like a man instead of a boy. Second, my sex hormones, hitherto dormant, would switch on and I would discover girls. I could only imagine, as a prepubescent boy, the relief I would feel when nature finally flipped that hormone switch, when at last I would begin to slaver and tremble over pictures of breasts in dog-eared copies of *Playboy*, stashed lovingly under my bed. I looked forward to it.

Reader, I do not doubt that you will be as surprised and dismayed today as I was then when I tell you that this is not what happened. Or, as I saw things then, it was not *yet* what happened. My boyish muscle-tinglings did not subside into manly breast-cravings. Instead, they all out of nowhere arose from their prepubescent recumbency and, like a mouse turning into a raging bear, they swallowed me whole. They did so in the person of Paul.

He was a boy of middling height, where I was short. He

had darkish skin with a bit of olive color in it, where I was pale. He had light-brown hair on his arms that turned tawny gold in the summer sunlight, where I was smooth. He was competent at sports, where I was a bumbler. He had a heavy, dense bone structure, where mine was very small and light. He had thick, powerful hands, where mine were skeletal and soft. He was not particularly handsome: even I never saw him as handsome. But he was strong! Paul at fourteen was a boy with a man's strength. The eighth-grade health book contained a picture of a brawny workman's arm, holding a stack of boards aloft. I spent a good many slow lessons contemplating that arm. Paul, I saw, actually possessed it. He could bear me aloft with it as though I were a doll (I imagined). His thick right hand could envelop mine in a handshake and crush it. I began to think about him day and night.

Not only him, let me add. In high school I craned my neck for glimpses of Bill Jones's thighs, Bob Demaine's forearms, and the plummy calves on that older boy whose name I never did know. In a peculiar way which seemed to fit well with the general weirdness of my preoccupations, I tended to fetishize particular bits of boys. Partly, I now believe, this was an evasive maneuver: by dividing erotic feelings into tiny packets, I could suppose that they were not erotic feelings at all. Much better to believe that I was merely envious of other boys' particular endowments. Among the many such endowments which I obsessively "envied," penile endowment was conspicuously missing. It never occurred to me to hanker to see another boy's cock, much less to want to touch it. I was fascinated and enslaved by all aspects of masculinity except the most blatant and unambiguous one. That omission, too, served a purpose. If I was not interested in penises, I could not be a homosexual, could I? I must instead be—well, a what?

What in the world was I? I pushed the question away. It pushed back. I pushed it away harder. It came back with redoubled force. I could only conclude, if I concluded anything, that I was a freak of nature. I had no sexual feelings, but instead was madly obsessive. I could not be a homosexual: I was not effeminate, I had no desire to be touched sexually by a man, indeed the concept mildly revolted me. But I was not behaving the way heterosexuals behaved. If I thought about it, I saw that there was no place on earth for me. I was otherworldly.

So, understandably, I tried not to think about it. Instead I did what has since become known as compartmentalizing. In one compartment was my rock-solid belief that I had no sexual feelings at all. In the other compartment was: Paul. Day in, day out, Paul. Paul was a standing reminder that I was nothing like normal, yet I was not even provided the grace of being normally abnormal. Paul was more difficult to rationalize than Bill Jones's thighs, because I did not fetishize just a few bits of him: I fetishized all the bits of him (except, always except, that one forbidden part). Toward the beginning, when I was about fourteen, my attention was seized by his hand. One day he pushed a piece of paper along the floor toward me. When I picked it up, I found a handprint. It might as well have been a pornographic drawing. I was astonished, riveted. I tried to stretch my hand over it and found that his broad palm easily eclipsed mine and his fingers were oaks to my weed stalks. From the hand, my attention quickly grew in compass until Paul loomed in all respects, in every particular, as a physical superman. No, as Superman. As Sinbad Jr. But flesh and blood, and two rows away from me in Spanish class! I began drinking him in, feasting upon fantasies of his strength. I had no idea why, or even what it was I was doing. I had not acquired this new obsession, which dwarfed all earlier ones: it had acquired me.

I am always bitterly amused when I hear people say homosexuality is a choice. Even many otherwise thoughtful people maintain that the homosexual is a heterosexual who perversely ignores, or at least somehow represses, his natural cravings. I say "otherwise thoughtful" because I know of no position which collapses more quickly, under even a moment's examination, than this one. Never mind the obvious question of why anyone would choose homosexuality, with all the inconveniences and confusions and difficulties it poses. Let us suppose, for argument's sake, that there are people who declare "Actually, I would prefer to be (probably) childless, to face a hundred kinds of social difficulties, to disappoint and maybe horrify my parents, to risk alienating myself from some of my friends and many of my peers, to be an object of disgust and scorn to many millions of people. Sure. Sounds fun." Let us also overlook, again for argument's sake, that many homosexuals, far from embracing their condition, struggle desperately to change or suppress it, even to the point of suicide. No: imagine that homosexuality is something many people contemplate and choose. Now arises the question: Suppose (I want to ask heterosexuals) you decided, at age fourteen, to fall desperately in love with a classmate of your own sex. How would you go about doing it? How would you talk your temples into throbbing and your throat into constricting? How might you arrange to get a stone-hard erection, all out of nowhere, whenever you touch the image of a certain young man's strong hand? That handprint made my face hot, my throat tight, and my penis hard. How would you set about having such a reaction to a handprint, if you had "decided" one day it was a good idea? What hormonal levers would you pull?

    I do not maintain that all aspects of human sexuality are innate from birth and merely switch on biologically when the time comes. Far from it: that cannot be true. It is not uncommon for one of a pair of identical twins (genetic clones) to be homosexual and the other heterosexual. I know such a pair myself. (And neither of the two has the least doubt about the direction of his orientation.) The existence of sexually disjunctive twin pairs tells us for a certainty that sexuality, while clearly having a large heritable component, is not wholly determined by genes. It is determined by genes and something else. My own experience, moreover, leaves me in no doubt about two things. First, that I was definitely disposed toward homosexuality from a very early age. Second, that the particular course my sexuality took was partly determined by what happened to me day by day after birth. Imagine, for an analogy, a stream of water. It "wants" to flow downhill, and one way or another will always eventually do so; but the particular path it takes will depend upon a thousand facts of happenstance: the presence of a rock here, soft soil there, an animal track which becomes a channel, a channel which eventually becomes a gorge. I cannot imagine flowing in any direction but "downhill," toward an eroticism directed at masculinity. But, oh, the twists, the kinks! I felt weak, and so I fetishized strength. I could not bear the notion that I might be a homosexual, and so, rather than entertaining that idea, I let my attentions focus upon all aspects of masculinity except the single most blatant one. And, of course, the appearance of Paul was happenstance. If not Paul, it would have been someone else. But the fact that it was he whom I lit upon fixed, in turn, the expression of my sexuality. Predisposition and personality and experience all met and reacted like explosive gasses in a hot chamber. I could, with desperate struggle, contain the explosion or divert some of its force below ground. Throughout, however, I was aware of myself as helpless to direct what was happening to me. "Choose" to spend days in school and nights in bed thinking about, dreaming about, gazing upon Paul? Just so does the dragonfly choose the winds which whip it in a hurricane.

Thinking about him, of course, was not enough. I needed to suck him up, breathe him in, know what it might mean to be like him. I wanted to be around him. I wanted to *be* him. And so, on the playground and in the classroom and eventually after school, I pushed myself forward toward friendship. He turned out to have a friendly disposition. He was bright, amiable, easygoing. More, he was unsuspicious. He seemed to like having me as a friend and never seemed to imagine that, even as we studied and chatted together, I was at every moment feeling the power that surged toward me from his body. I say *seemed*, because I must have made it hard for him not to notice, and also because he did exactly as I dreamed he might. He began building his body, noticing it, nurturing it. At first he talked about doing gymnastics. After all, he had the strength. No, no, I said, trying to sound only casually interested. You have so much natural talent for weight lifting. Wouldn't it be a shame not to develop it, not to be all you can? At every moment, telling him this, I was thinking: *Please! Please! Please!* Paul, born with the gift of brawn, growing bigger and bigger, stronger and stronger, till no ordinary sleeve could contain his arms. And me beside him, watching him flex his growing muscles and reveling in his changing shape. To think of this was almost too much.

He did it, and I "helped" him. By this time, I was on intimate terms with bodybuilding magazines, and had found a newsstand downtown that carried them (they were still unusual, and somewhat peculiar, in those days). Once a month, making sure to be vague about where I was going, I would walk 20 minutes to the No. 40 bus stop and ride half an hour downtown, hungrily seize the latest issue of *Muscle Builder* (what a title!), and spirit it home in a brown bag, to be stashed in that cabinet next to my bed. Pornography is as pornography does. I would have hidden away a postcard of the Mona Lisa if it had had the effect upon me of those muscle magazines. It seemed likely to me that anyone who saw a nerd like me with a muscle magazine would instantly put two and two together, leaving me stuttering with shame. I mean, why else would a weak, skinny boy have bodybuilding magazines, except to feed obsessive, fetishistic cravings? Paul, unlike me, made no secret of his interest in muscles. He had begun to work out and to grow. He liked, mirabile dictu, to talk about his progress, so long as he was not suspected of boasting. And I, thanks to my many trips to the newsstand downtown, was just the one to discuss the finer points with him.

How many sets? How many reps? How much are you bench-pressing this week? Have you tried inclines? I bought a little weight set, but got no results. Actually, I was hardly trying. I knew the natural order of things: Paul was springing into manhood, and those new muscles were a young man's body pushing out through his molting skin; I was a boy, too immature to grow muscles or, by the way, to have sexual feelings. I was a late bloomer, always looking a few years younger than most of my classmates. Having no immediate prospect of changing from boyish caterpillar to manly butterfly, I redoubled my solicitousness of one who was metamorphosing before my eyes. Reader, I was the world's most appreciative audience. I studied every phase of Paul's development. In the afternoons, after we had finished our math, I would beg him to show me his biceps, to strip off his shirt and let me comment sagely on the progress of his chest, to detail each one of his new feats of strength. By the time he was sixteen, he had muscles you could see through clothing. He tossed big plates onto iron bars and made pushing them around look natural. He entered (though did not win) a power-lifting contest or two, and a bodybuilding contest. One day I saw him lift and easily swing a heavy pick which I could barely hoist. If I pressed him—always prying for more, yet trying not to seem *too* interested—he might tell me how he performed dozens of dips, or how tight his old shirts were getting and how that sensation of increasing tightness felt to him, or how someone had noticed his physique and asked whether he lifted weights. On hearing each new detail,

DENIAL

I vibrated like a plucked string, or a plucked chicken. And all the while, sitting next to him at the study table, I would watch hawkishly for that moment when the short sleeve slipped upward to reveal baseball biceps. I noticed how the Arizona sunshine glinted off the hairs on the backs of his broad hands. Once in a while I brushed up against him, coincidentally you understand, and I gulped at his hardness.

Eventually I talked him into letting me go to the gym with him. This was nervy of me. I was scared of the awesome masculinity of a gym and sure that a 100-pound boy would be laughed at, or, worse, that "they" might guess why I was really there. Paul had his doubts about being accompanied by a fan club and Greek chorus. I was not, you see, going to lift weights myself, for I was intimidated by the sweat and camaraderie of men, and certain of being ridiculed. No: I was going to supervise, advise, "help." "Helping" meant helpfully commenting on the impressive gains Paul was making, helpfully urging him to flex and pose and show "us" this or that muscle, and helpfully now and then putting a hand or an arm on a weight or on him, feeling the straining of his body under his T-shirt, absorbing his dampness through my pores. Then afterward I would urge him—objectively, for his own sake, so that he could assess his progress—to peel off the shirt and twist and tighten before the mirror while I noted the slabs on the upper chest or the thickening shoulders or the eye-popping forearms. This was an injection of adrenaline directly into a vein. I would jauntily say goodbye to him, dash home, close the bedroom door, and feverishly replay every moment, trying to recall each feat of strength and burn into my mind every blessed glistening curve, the better to adore it.

I wonder what his parents thought, if anything. His father was a genial engineer who loved to tell a good story and regularly took Paul hiking in the Grand Canyon. His mother was sweet and likable. But she played Oral Roberts on the radio, and they were churchgoing Christians of the true-believing variety. We liked each other, his parents and I. But then, I don't imagine that either ever turned to the other and said, "Say, honey, don't you feel that that boy is showing an unhealthy interest in our son?" As for Paul, I'm sure he thought my interest peculiar. But there is a charming symbiosis between heterosexual vanity and homosexual infatuation. No girl could have said to him the things that I did about his body; no girl could have noticed in the minutely attentive yet seemingly detached way I did. And he was glad of my friendship and seemed to take it at face value. Perhaps he sensed my raging obsession but concluded that it did not matter so long as nothing "happened"; or perhaps—who knows?—he wanted something to happen. If he did want that, however, he was in for a disappointment. I would have been appalled at the notion of making any sexual move in his direction; if he had made any move toward me, I would have told him I had no interest in such a thing. For my fascination with him, I was certain, was *not sexual in nature*. This was not, or mostly not, a self-deception. I knew with certainty I was not a homosexual. I did not feel like a homosexual; certainly I never once saw, or tried to see, Paul's privates. I never viewed our friendship in a remotely sexual context. He just seemed to have an inexplicable, bizarre effect on me: that was all.

I, of course, felt intensely the strange and exploitive aspect of my friendship with Paul. Although I liked him, I was driven to like him by my desire to bathe in and feed upon his radioactive physical emanation. Even if he did not wonder about my forever badgering him for a glimpse of balled-up biceps, I felt a need to reassure him that our friendship was innocent. On several occasions, when I was seventeen or eighteen, I undertook to explain to him exactly what was going on.

I have no trouble recalling what I told him. You see, I said, I am a small, skinny guy. I've always been self-conscious about being so small and weak, and I've wanted to be bigger and stronger. But I don't have the kind of natural size and strength you have. I look at you and think: *There's a guy with potential! There's the sort of person I'd want to be but am not.* I see your physique (I said), and you have incredible natural thickness and strength (here I would have been careful not to get carried away). And so I think, *If I can't have a great physique, at least I can help you do it—and anyone with that kind of gift should make the most of it.* And so I vicariously enjoy seeing you work to your potential. (I specifically recall using the word *vicariously*.) So if I sometimes seem pushy about asking you to pose or take measurements, that's why. And Paul just nodded, as if to say "Whatever." He seemed to find my compulsion to explain myself more peculiar than either my behavior or the explanation itself. He did not mind, really, talking about his body, within reason. He did not mind letting me admire it, within bounds. He actually liked it, and it did us both good in a happy friendship (and in those days I was the best friend he had: devoted and then some). It was just I who was wracked and baffled.

4

AH, EXPLANATIONS. I told you some pages ago that I had begun, on the doorstep of adolescence, to work out a theory of what was happening to me; but I have ducked setting it before you in all its convoluted glory, partly because it is unpleasant to recall, partly because it is so laborious, twisting back upon itself in a perfect tangle of self-confirmation. I have written many books and articles, some on complicated subjects. None approaches the baroque complexity of my youthful self-"explanation." Newton's *Principia* and Aquinas's *Summa*, I sometimes think, must pale in intricacy beside my "explanation." Time, then, to set forth this quantum mechanics of soullessness.

I also promised to embarrass you. Perhaps I have done that already. The fixation on Paul, however, does not greatly embarrass me. All-consuming as it was then, in retrospect it was nothing more unusual than a major teenage crush, prolonged and deepened by the absence of anything like the prospect of a grown-up sexual love to supplant it. It was a silly thing, a hormonal madness, but teenagers are silly. No, for me what is harder to reveal is the self which I built to contain and "rationalize" my then-incomprehensible feelings. What I have told you so far is merely homosexuality, and the particular way in which it awoke and unfurled in me. What I reveal next is inversion. I only beg you to remember that what I will show you looks as strange to me now as it no doubt does to you; but that in those days it seemed utterly, inescapably natural.

In the face of my own obviously weird behavior, I had recourse to several different strategies for coping. For a long time, as I've mentioned, the best one was to try to ignore what was going on and wait until I became normal, which of course would happen when I got old enough, just as it had happened to all the adults I saw around me. Until my teens, I just went with the flow, enjoying my Superman jollies and the physical tingling they brought me. Even through my early twenties, I clung to a faint hope that somehow I might still turn out normal. But Paul, while not quite exterminating my hope, was catastrophic for my complacency. Instead of simmering down, my bizarre behavior boiled up. Instead of converging with an ordinary young-male sexuality, it veered wildly away. As fourteen turned to fifteen and fifteen to sixteen, I began to realize that I was like a man on a slow boat to the South Pole, looking glumly aft as the shores of home vanished beyond the horizon.

    Well, I was no slacker when it came to working things out. So I applied myself to understanding what kind of boat I might be on. I knew that I had strong feelings about males, muscles, strength. Actually, I had more than "strong feelings" by then: I had an overwhelming physical reaction, the sort of reaction which blurs the very distinction, so prized by Catholic theologians, between sexual "orientation" and sexual "behavior." In addition to that rather clear evidence, I also knew that I myself was not at all like the men and boys who thrilled and tortured me. I was small and thin and weak and awkward. So what might it be that drove me to fits of gulping and gaping distraction in the presence of, say, Bill Jones's bare thighs, which were so unlike my own? Clearly the answer was as I had long suspected: envy. I must be envious.

    There were, it seemed to me, two classes of young human males: mortals and gods. The main difference was that the gods made me burn with that searing inner fire. Just to see their broad-shouldered graceful carriages and handsome faces and shiny hair and well-knit tigerish bodies made my heart beat and my stomach burn with a feeling which could not be desire and so must be resentment, jealousy. Between such as them and such as me stood an impassable, unbridgeable gulf. They knew who they were and I knew who I was, and never would I possess an ounce of that golden charm of the effortlessly manly. Their very effortlessness, in fact, was the most gratuitous of insults: although they were gods, they took their fantastic endowment of masculine majesty for granted! They were like sighted people whose supreme endowment of vision could be appreciated only by a blind man. They could never understand how sublimely gifted they were, because they could never conceive of how utterly bereft I was. And of course—a final injustice—I could not tell them about their gift. I could not express my abject awe of their inborn and unquestioned masculinity. That would be weird, it would be fawning, it would be incomprehensible to them. If I ever allowed myself to say, as I always wanted to do, "My God, Bill, your legs are the eighth wonder of the world," he would look at me with incredulity or even disgust. Among all the gods, there was only one, Paul, whose praises I could sing aloud; and he could accept my paeans only on condition that I pretended not to care. Normal boys could trade stories about the glories of Cynthia's breasts, which she used as paperweights, or of the legs that made Cathy the standout of the cheerleading squad. They could *speak*. I could express nothing, or nothing intelligible. So there I was, a solitary, blind creature unable even to extol the wonder of sight: blind *and* dumb.

It was not the god-men I resented, really, but my own fate in being forever excluded from their number. And even my envy of them, I realized, further separated me from them: really masculine boys didn't chew their insides out over their own want of masculinity. You could not (I assumed) qualify as a member of the gods' club if you hankered to get in. In my isolation, I saw that I was alone in my obsession with the mystery of manhood. Many boys were not actually gods; but it never occurred to them to obsessively "envy" their betters. I was different in that respect, too. I viewed every well-made young male as a personal rebuke. Every superior specimen of a young man was not just a god in his own right, but a standing repudiation of me, a reminder of all that I could never hope to be. I began to realize, by the time I was about fifteen or sixteen, that there were three classes of young man, not two. There were the masculine gods, so unselfconsciously and enviably magnificent; there were the regular boys, so unselfconsciously and blessedly ordinary. And there was also a third class, a category for boys who would be grateful even to be unselfconsciously ordinary, so that they could be released from their prison of sullen envy. The third class consisted of me. I occupied it alone.

Alone, of course, in my secret coils of "envy." And alone, even more, in my sexlessness. It did not escape me—oh, I was a keen one—that many other boys were beginning to explore the flowering of a maturing sexuality. Some very lucky and precocious boys actually lost their virginity. Many others were holding hands and kissing and generally getting on with the business of growing up. Me, I waited and waited, but no sexual awakening would come. No girlfriend, no desire for a girlfriend, no desire to touch a girl, no interest in anything feminine, nothing. I carried a painful memory of a birthday party when I was in third or fourth grade: the other boys had run off together up a mountain path, but I couldn't keep up, and stayed behind with the adults. Here I was being left behind again. Tinkerbell was going from boy to boy, bringing each one sexually alive with a touch of her dew-dipped wand. But she had forgotten me! I saw I was in danger of being a perpetual child: a eunuch.

In no small measure, I suspected, this was my own fault. Even to me, it seemed unlikely that I, alone among the millions and millions of young men, had come down by happenstance with some hitherto unknown tropical disease which denied me any form of proper sexuality but left me otherwise completely healthy. Surely, if such a thing happened in this world, I would have heard something about it. No: I must have been getting something wrong. But what? Ah, this must be it: I wasn't trying hard enough.

I had, you see, a theory of heterosexuality. My theory was designed to explain how it might be possible for heterosexuality to exist—as the evidence around me suggested it probably did—while still allowing for the possibility that I myself was heterosexual. No conventional theory would fulfill this challenging mission. If, after all, heterosexuality was a strong and innate erotic attraction to the opposite sex, then I did not (yet—always not *yet!*) appear to be a heterosexual. Moreover, and more compelling: to me, a strong and innate erotic attraction to women or girls was quite inconceivable. Unlike some homosexual males, I never felt even a fleeting passion for women. Not once did I stare at a girl's budding breasts with wonder, or tingle at the thought of her alone in the shower. I could no more imagine longing to touch a woman than longing to touch a toaster. In fact, I was well along in my twenties before I became really convinced that heterosexual men felt, or possibly could feel, as passionately attracted to women as I was to men. (I mean, how *could* they?) So, when I was in my mid-teens, the standard model of heterosexuality not only excluded me, it seemed farfetched to begin with. Bright boy that I was, I figured out a more plausible model: *heterosexuality was a learned behavior.* One began, perhaps, with the slightest small tickle of interest in a woman and, with determined effort and plenty of practice, nurtured it until it grew at last to the fullness of an appropriately vigorous lust. I winced at first when I sipped beer, but people told me that as I grew accustomed to it I would come to like it. Of course, some boys liked beer right off the bat, but for those who did not—most, probably—beer was an acquired taste, developed through use. Sex, it stood to reason, was like that: after a rough and uncertain start, you got to rather like it once you developed a taste for it.

Then, eventually, it would come to seem the most natural, even compelling, thing in the world. At that point, you had become a grown-up. Q.E.D.

You can see where my theory left me. Practice makes perfect, and I had not begun to practice. I was the boy who never learned to swim, because he was afraid to jump into the pool. The reason I felt no desire for girls was that I had never done anything with them. But—you see this coming—the reason I had never done anything was because I felt no desire for them. The only way out of my hole and into the game, then, was to do what all the boys around me were doing: close my eyes, hold my nose, repress my natural fear and distaste, and do something with a girl. Amazingly, I never really took seriously the possibility that boys necking with girls in the parking lot might actually be driven by their instincts, rather than forcing themselves to learn sex as if doing their homework. Instead, I assumed they had the guts to do what I could not. So there I was again, a weakling and a coward: unmasculine. Which, of course, explained why not many girls showed much interest in me anyway.

It fit the facts, my model. The reason I so resented masculine boys was that I was too sniveling to do as they did. My failure was moral. And I'm not finished yet.

One of the things I "envied" in other boys my age was the blossoming, not just of sexual maturity, but of physical maturity. Here again, there was a clear line, and I was on the wrong side of it. The line divided boys, who were dainty, soft creatures not so unlike girls, from men, who radiated that dangerous power of masculinity. Men were clad in hair and muscles and big-boned confidence. Paul had a man's strength and, soon enough, a man's body. I adored his body—meaning, I burned with "envy" of it. Likewise I "envied" Greg Spicer's precocious beard, and the tawny grown-up hair on Bill Jones's legs, and the mature tufts of dense black hair that peeked around the armholes of Bob Crowfoot's tank top. All were diplomas signifying graduation into that wonderful thing, manhood. I had none of them. I looked younger than my age. I had no use for a razor, little body hair, none of the muscular weight that distinguishes men from boys. Once again, I had been left behind. I was like a snake that had failed to molt, a boy unable to shed his skin and emerge a young man. Until manhood came, I would not attract girls, and I would not be inclined to experiment with them. I could not then learn sexuality until—when?

I reassured myself that the day would come, probably soon, and from manhood I would someday look back upon my teenage anxiety as a peculiar stage which I, like everyone, got through. But I believed my reassurances only on, if you will, odd-numbered days. Intuition told me that what I was feeling could not, in fact, be a variation of the standard prelude to a normal adulthood. It told me that boys went through something awkward, but not *this*. It did not, on those days when I listened, allow me to believe that I was merely behind or arrested physically, and therefore a coward with girls. More likely, it whispered, the other way around. The cowardice and the failure to feel stirred by females, I realized, seemed fundamental. I could not be a swashbuckler, a make-out artist, while still being me. (And in that supposition, at least, I was right: I did not have it in me to be heterosexual.) And so, on my comparatively truthful even-numbered days, I allowed myself to consider the possibility that the causality of my retardation flowed in both directions. That is: the reassuring version of things was that I was sexually retarded because I was physically arrested, in which case time and growth should eventually do the trick. Darkly, however, I suspected that the converse was also true: I was physically stunted because I was sexually retarded. *Because* I was a coward, I was also a eunuch, failing to take the positive steps which could unlock the hormones to make me a man. I had heard of tribal societies in which boys were initiated into sex in rites of passage. Desperately I imagined that such an initiation might somehow befall me. Some older woman would make a project of me, taking me in hand and starting the ball rolling at last. She might gently, oh so gently, bring me along one blessed day, showing me where to put my hand and what to do, and after my nervousness had subsided, passion for her breasts and her lips would begin to course through me, tentatively at first and then in a flood. And the flood would make a man of me finally; the long wait in this cave of echoing silence would be over.

But of course the truth, as I well knew, was that even if some knowing and sympathetic woman volunteered to show me the ropes, I would flee from her in horror. That was the whole problem. I was trapped between fear of girls and "envy" of boys, each feeding the other and devouring me between them. I was becalmed, dead center between the two. Because I did nothing, there was nothing I could do. There was no prospect of being, or even looking like, a grown-up, because I could not find the courage.

I began to tailspin. I loathed my boy's appearance, which left me stuck behind the rest of the world. But that was not all I loathed. When I was sixteen or seventeen, it dawned on me that this cacophonous mess—my boiling "envy" of jocks and manly boys, my fetishizing of muscles and hands, my paralysis in seducing girls, my missing or retarded sexuality, my inability to be normal or to enjoy any typical sort of adolescent awakening—all of it had a root cause. Logically, I saw that great envy must stem from a great difference. What kind of difference could be so great? Nothing was sufficient for the task except this: I was a sort of mutant.

Silently but meticulously, I catalogued my defects. I began with my feet. They were thin—much too thin, absurdly, monstrously thin, like the rest of me. Most boys wore shoes of average width, "D" width. They took their normal feet for granted and didn't even know that shoes came in widths! Whereas I—of course I, always I, inevitably I—took a narrow width, a "problem" size. The shoes most stores sold wouldn't fit me. I needed *special* shoes. I noted, too, my low arches. I was fond of noticing how others might languorously, gracefully, extend a leg and point the toes; my flat arch let me do no such thing. Press my foot down as far as I might, and it still stuck out at a sloppy right angle from the shin. This deformity, I supposed, might help account for my woeful calves, which I next considered. "Mosquito legs," a camp counselor had once called them, having no idea that his jape would burn for years. I had inherited my father's pipe-stem calves. When other boys crossed their legs, their calves pushed out to fill their jeans. Me, I was ashamed to wear shorts.

I was bowlegged, I realized. I got that from my father, too. I had pimples, and sometimes they left scars. *Of course* I would have pimples! I was short. My skin was sallow instead of ruddy. My skinny hands were weaker than most girls', my fingers so thin that I could not wear a class ring. (I was so confident I could not wear a ring that I never bothered getting fitted for one.) My tiny, fragile wrists, I saw, were too small to bear a man's wristwatch. For me, it would need to be a woman's watch, which of course meant no watch at all. My chest, hairless as an éclair, was reed-like. Other boys of sixteen were in men's shirts. Not me! My back—oh, worst of all. It confirmed the curse. From the time I was ten or eleven, adults would tell me to stand up straight. But I *am* standing up straight, I would miserably reply. I had eyes. I could see that something was wrong with my back. It was too curved, almost hunched. I knew it was true, and when no one believed me, I took myself to an orthopedist, who made X-rays. "Kyphosis," he declared: a backwards-bulging curvature of the spine. Nothing to be done about it, he said: it was a spinal deformity, actually pretty mild, in my case. I begged to differ. It was not at all mild. No, it meant I would forever look spidery, hunched. There were other skinny boys (though few if any in my league, I bitterly reflected), other pale boys, other boyish boys. But they did not have *this*! *This* was especially reserved for me, so that I might be the real article, a genuine horror show, suitable for a carnival booth.

Oh, I'm not done yet. I have not mentioned my oversized ears, or my overbite, which left me with a tiny chin and gave me the puckered triangular face of a locust. My second toe stuck out beyond my big toe; what was *that* about? There was more, but I will stop now. On careful consideration, I concluded that my eyebrows were nice, my hair tolerable, and my shoulders promising. But that was all. At every opportunity, I would stand next to Paul or put my arm alongside his and I would marvel in dumb, sour amazement that God should have built both Paul's arm and mine and chosen, as a kind of sadistic joke, to put both of us on the same planet.

The Creator had systematically stripped from me all the marks of masculinity that are a man's birthright: the feet and calves and thighs and hand and forearms and chest and back and jaw and skin and muscle and, yes, even the lust.

Sometimes, while I was reading or studying, the heat of "envy" would surge up in me and I would lose my concentration. Visions of Paul's forearm would spring up vividly before me, or his hand or his thick chest. "My God," I would think, "to have *that*! To experience *that*!" But then I would recall that I did not and could not have *that*, that *this* was my fate. A crescendo began, a swelling of loathing which, I now imagine, may have helped both to explain and to quell another sort of swelling. To be rid of this monstrous, skinny, even ludicrous body! To put a stop to the humiliating joke! One day, interrupted by an onslaught of "envy" while reading in bed, I followed the fantasy along. I looked at my arms and legs and hands and feet and began to imagine hacking them off. I would get no replacement set, but at least I would not have to look at these! I would hack off my ludicrous limbs and have them hurled into a pit, into the sea. Chop, chop, chop. Then would the loathing end? Would the "envy" die down? Would it stop shaking and heaving and twisting me, without this freakish body to mock me? For God's sake, could I not then be, at least, human, crippled but human? I imagined looking down at myself and seeing normal limbs and feet and hands. Better to be any normal person than this!

No wonder, then, that I ached to live vicariously through Paul, thrilling to every sight of his skin or frame. In my own disgraceful container, how could I not yearn to enfold myself in a man's mantle?

In hindsight, I see I was a candidate for what some psychologists now call body dysmorphic disorder, an obsessively distorted and negative body-image—though that diagnosis had not, in my youth, been invented (and is still little known). When I look now at photos from that period, I see a boy who indeed looks young for his age and quite thin and delicate, with a mild but noticeable slouch. I certainly was not inventing all of that: it was true. On the other hand, the boy who looks back in pictures has a pleasing, sweet-natured face, soft brown eyes, a rich thatch of wavy brown hair, decent if unathletic proportions. No one would mistake the boy in the picture for a jock. But he is neither hideous nor even homely. I could look in the mirror even then and see that what looked back was, in fact, not a mantis or a mutant. Yet—how to explain this, even to myself?—my appearance as reflected objectively was beside the point. I might look halfway human in this mirror or in that photo, at this moment or in that light, but that trivial victory had no bearing on the unbudgeable reality of my ugliness and sexlessness. My deformity was a fact whose certainty transcended any possible evidence to the contrary. Besides, the only mirror whose reflection one really feels, rather than sees, is the social mirror: the reaction of others. I saw that no one noticed me, no one desired me, that my position in life was always to be admiring and never admired. What was any picture compared with that? A whole chorus of comforters could not have penetrated my conviction that I was abnormal. I positively depended on my "abnormality" to explain my "envy." Without it, I was inexplicable.

Writing this now, it all sounds crazy. What I must somehow remember, and ask a reader somehow to understand, is that it was a struggle for rationality in the face of what seemed to be utterly inexplicable circumstances. If I was ghastly and deformed, then I could reasonably be obsessed with athletic boys and muscular men; therefore I could be sane. Whereas if I was not ghastly and deformed, then my consuming obsessions were nothing but bizarre, crazy fixations that led nowhere—not even to homosexuality, since I had no desire to "do" anything. Moreover, I could cling to the hope that I would shed my misshapen boyishness with time, become a man, and be normal. Shedding my sexuality would have seemed less certain.

In short, my inversion, grotesque as it was, held together a crazily integrated world, if only with Scotch tape and staples. It kept me going, kept me calm. It was, at the time, the best I could do with the facts available. It forestalled any direct confrontation with the troll in the cellar, any reckoning with the possibility that I might be one of *them*, and not one of *us*.

DENIAL

In a curious way, by allowing me to get through every day without acknowledging that I *was* fully alive sexually, and that *this* was in fact my sexuality in full bloom, my inversion kept me together until the time finally came when I could face the truth. In a way, I marvel at the ingenuity of a boyish mind that could defend itself so elaborately from a reality it could neither face nor flee. I could, through my inversion, lie to Paul and lie to me and, lo and behold, it was not a lie! It was truth, but through Alice's looking glass, seen complete in every particular, yet reading back to front and bottom to top. By being an invert, I could avoid being a pervert. At the time, it was the only choice I had.

But at a price. I was a boy without love or sexual passion, or any prospect of love or passion, in a world awash with youthful eros. Other boys had juvenile romances; I had my homework and my debating practice and my full-time, professional self-loathing. In one respect, what I suspected then was true, though not in precisely the way I believed: so long as I was an invert, I could not be a grown-up, because adult passion and adult pursuit of an erotic other were submerged and squelched. Men do not "envy"; they love. They open their hearts and let a torrent of longing rush out into the world, and upon that torrent they lurch into an unknown and unbounded future of turbulence and despair and elation and, in the end, commitment. None of that could so much as begin for me, not as long as I was a goony soft-eyed boy woefully enslaved by the golden hairs on the backs of Paul's oaken wrists, unworthy to share his planet. My inverted world made a kind of tautological sense, yes, but I was trapped in it, trapped in what I vaguely understood, even then, to be my own childhood.

5

YOU WON'T believe me, but through it all, I had a fairly glorious rest-of-my-life. Psychologically speaking, the whole point of an inversion is to label, defuse, and above all contain what otherwise threatens to overwhelm. Understanding that I was a physically ghastly specimen who naturally envied all superior boys, I was free to go on with other things. Even then, I somehow gathered that a kind of great darkness or reckoning lay ahead—of what kind, I could not imagine—but for now, for the foreseeable future, I would simply swallow my abnormality and move forward.

So I worked hard in my classes and earned exemplary grades. I took piano lessons and decided to become a concert pianist and then, when that turned out to involve actual talent, perhaps a conductor instead, which, unfortunately, also involved talent. I joined the debate team, and participated with the kind of full-throttle abandon that other boys reserved for sports. Before I was finished, I was the team captain and state champion, traveling to tournaments as far away as Berkeley. I joined the choir and sang as loudly as I could, which was pretty loudly. I wrote a setting of Shelley's "Hymn of Pan" for four-part chorus and piano, which promising composition, to my eternal disappointment, was never premiered or even heard by human ears, despite having been based on a perfectly good pop tune filched from the radio. I ran for student-body office and lost, but not before decorating the campus with signs announcing that I was the choice of the Grand Rabbi. (Why that slogan did not work, I still cannot fathom.) I had as many friends as most boys my age, and was elected president of our National Honor Society, whereupon I announced that our main and indeed only constitutional imperative was to honor ourselves at parties and picnics. I went to movies in shopping malls and drove around town late at night in cars with too many people in them. Summers, I worked for my father and then for a local typesetting company, read stacks of books, took courses, went to midnight showings of *The Rocky Horror Picture Show*, and decided to become acquainted with the string quartets of Bartok, having read somewhere that they were the century's finest chamber music (good enough for me). I read the papers and worried diligently about the energy crisis and wondered why good people went on allowing bad people to run the world. In hindsight, the great joke was not that I was such an abnormal teenager of my type and class, but that I was such a banal and ordinary one. Even my obsessions were, in their way, the trite stuff of adolescence: how many teenagers, after all, pass through a period of frenzied vanity and self-consciousness and introspection? Or, rather, how many do not?

Maybe, then, it is not so surprising that I was mostly pretty cheerful, even in my misery. Sometimes the molten undercurrent of "envy" and self-loathing would flash up and flood me with shuddering self-revulsion. Mostly, however, it burbled and boiled down below, like a sulfurous hot spring in the basement. It was always down there, and I was never out of range of its stench and its heat and its sometimes nauseating vapors, but I was usually able to tread around it, and I could hide it from everybody else. Thanks, in no little part, to my inversion, life went on.

When I was fifteen, I became dimly aware, through my haze of self-absorption, that a girl liked me. From the start, I foresaw problems. For one, she was just a freshman. I was a lordly sophomore, and to me she was but a child. For another, she had thick ankles and didn't seem very pretty. No doubt for that reason, I did not feel excited by her. I did not feel anything, really. For a little while, she and I hung out together. Once or twice, I ventured to hold her hand, on the assumption that hand-holding was expected. But her too-sincere glances and her freshman giggles told me she was not a going item for me. Too immature. We drifted apart.

A year or two later, I met Mary. She sat at the desk behind mine in American History, was a few months older than I, very bright, and laughed heartily and often. She was a violinist, and we chatted about music, and she laughed charitably at my wisecracks. Soon we were friendly enough so that the teacher remarked one day that we made a congenial pair: and we did. I spent more and more time with her, mostly at her house, which seemed an oasis compared with the stress of my own. My parents were divorced, my mother had left years earlier, my father was a single parent juggling three children, a legal career, and everything else. Mary had two parents at home, both of them warm and welcoming people, her father a Presbyterian minister, her mother a teacher. At their dinner table, I filled in for Mary's older sister, who was away at college. Those evenings at dinner, after Mary and I had studied for a while and talked for a while, took on a rosy glow for me, the glow of an ordinary family life. Afterward, we would go back to her room and she would give me a report on her troubled heart, and I would nod sagely and offer comfort and advice and, in due course, hold her hand. Mary, teenager that she was, had her share of troubles. Her parents, so kind to me, bickered with each other and worried about her; she felt confined in that suburban house; she was, above all, lonely, too inward to make friends easily but not so inward as to not need them. I did not, however, understand why she was unhappy, and it did not occur to me then that I was unable to provide what she needed most. As far as I was concerned, we were the best of friends. What else, after all, would we be? I felt no spark with Mary, no impulse to hold or caress her. I felt kindly toward her, as an older brother might, and stayed aloof from her, as an older brother might. We talked about her parents, her school, her life—I was not about to tell her what was on my mind (Paul). As she opened her heart, I offered her my keenest philosophical insights, of which I had quite a few. I explained to her the need to be stoical and independent, the meaning of happiness, and the importance of oneness with one's self in attaining a state of true emotional transparency. I believe I must have behaved like a boy rabbi, or a teenage guru. I told her she was a good person, and I told her the meaning of goodness. (Spinoza was germane, I dimly recall.)

Of course—of course!—I said nothing of my "envy," nothing of the sulfur spring boiling in the basement. There seemed nothing to tell except everything, and everything was so much and so confused that it amounted to nothing. I was certainly not going to tell a young woman, of all people, about my desperate fear of sexuality—that is, about my seeming lack of any sexuality whatever. I was not about to tell a minister's daughter that the pictures in muscle magazines set my retinas afire, and that the briefest glance at Paul's explosive biceps made me tremble and sweat and squirm until I could rush home and relieve the tension. I did not keep all of this secret from her, in the way one might hide a misdemeanor or an illness; it just did not occur to me that my state could possibly be told or understood. There was simply nothing to be said, except to state bald facts which could lead only to incorrect conclusions. I was not hiding that part of myself from her: rather I was pretending, and in fact believed, that all of my strangeness was not me at all, but instead a kind of lunatic baggage which I would eventually shed.

I knew, though, what the world expected of me. Be a man! I was curious, too, and of course it was high time for me to get my feet wet. So, on a moonlit night, Mary and I walked through the desert to the banks of the canal and stood close together, and there, with the dry breeze tickling us, we drew ourselves into a stiff embrace, and I kissed her. And kissed her. I kissed her, it seemed, for a long, long time. Specifically, when I say I "kissed" her, I put my lips against hers and pressed them there and wagged my head gradually from side to side the way movie lovers do. Mainly I experienced difficulty breathing. My thoughts were a hundred miles away, pondering the situation with a puzzled detachment which I knew even at that moment to be ludicrous. *So now I am "necking," like the other boys, which must be terrific, and here are her lips and my lips and they are touching, eternally it seems, and what is it here that I am supposed to find interesting?* I was conscious after a while that I was bored and felt much as you might while waiting for a bus or an elevator. I was aware that something was supposed to happen next. Perhaps the point of kissing was not the pressing together of the lips but some natural sequel. However, nothing else seemed to happen. I might as well have been kissing the back of my own hand, or a doorknob. I felt oddly like a TV alien earnestly trying to understand what kissing means to earthlings, except that on TV, the alien who kisses the girl falls in love despite himself—such is the power of the kiss—whereas I was still as mystified as ever. Eventually, Mary and I took our lips apart and walked home. We probably tried it only once or twice again after that. I concluded that kissing was overrated.

I had not expected to be so disappointed. When I was thirteen or so, in summer camp, a kindly girls' counselor took it upon herself to teach me how to dance. She put on an Elton John record and showed me how to shake my body to the music. Then came a slower number, and she held me and we swayed. I think I came about up to her breastbone, so I was not conscious of much except the enfolding softness of her body, and the maternal corona of her maturity. I felt a surge of excitement as I realized that I was now, for the first time, doing this very adult thing. On the whole, I rather liked this business of dancing; and how much more likable kissing might be! Dancing, kissing, fucking, marriage, babies: I was on the first rung of nature's ladder from pleasure to adulthood. So far, so good. But the second rung, when it came, was not as promised. No bells or whistles, no gongs or chimes, not even a burp. Nothing. I decided that, on the one hand, I was not yet ready to kiss, and that, on the other hand, kissing was a dull preliminary which people saw in movies and thus felt obliged to push themselves through, like washing hands before a meal, prefatory to something more fun. I am not sure I can imagine what Mary thought of our kissing. I infer she didn't enjoy it much, either. One day, after about a year of our odd hovering in the space between friendship and romance, Mary asked if she could talk to me. Sure—anything—what? Well, she said, when we had plopped ourselves into two iron-framed '60s chairs in my living room. Well, what? Well, she had been thinking. She had noticed a coolness, an aloofness in my attitude toward her. More than that, she had noticed the way I looked at Paul. She thought, nothing personal, that I might be homosexual. Oh, I said. Gulp. And, she went on, she had discussed this with her parents, and they thought it not unlikely. They all thought maybe I should talk to someone.

Well. Well well well. I would tell you I flew into a panic or a rage or a convulsion of tears or, best of all, an access of self-revelation, but I did not. I was the rabbi right to the end. After the initial shock of the subject's coming up out of the blue, I was positively serene. I calmly told her that I was not homosexual. I had nothing against homosexuals, but I knew for certain I was not one. I said so with the sublime assurance of one who believes he knows what he is talking about, someone who is asserting the presence of his hand at the end of his arm. Nonetheless, she did not seem satisfied. Shortly after that, we had an argument over something trivial, and stopped spending time together. I saw nothing more of her parents, and not much of her. I was confident that Mary's assessment was groundless, and managed to hustle it straight back out through a side door. But I was mortified that such a judgment should have been made. And so wrongly!

Homosexuals often speak of "the closet": the intricate and soul-twisting web of lies and evasions which, down through the ages, they have woven to create the illusion that they are anything but homosexual, or at least to make denial plausible. In the outer closet, one knows the truth but struggles to maintain a false front before the larger world, which, on its side of the bargain, knows the truth but pretends to be taken in. In the inner closet, the delusion ensnares its weaver, at least to an extent. One tells oneself white lies and makes excuses to explain away the obvious. "Not homosexual—bisexual, maybe." "Just randy and feeling horny." "Just a phase." Yet there is a third place, a pre-closet place, the alien landscape of inversion, where excuses and evasions are so encompassing as to leave nothing to deny or hide. In this place, it is a dead certainty that one is not homosexual; and instead of turning oneself upside-down to fool the world, one turns the world upside-down to fool oneself. This third zone, in which confusion and evasion are so pervasive as to create a self-contained world of rational lunacy, is all but impenetrable. I can only liken it to absorption in a cult or a sect or an all-embracing ideology which answers all questions before they are properly asked, and seals off all doors to the outside, so that, indeed, one hardly imagines that there *is* an outside. Of course I knew that there was an outside, but I knew by deduction and inference, not by dint of any immediate contact with the outside itself. I also understood that life on the outside was unavailable to me. I could not love, I could not kiss, I had no passion, only resentment and a kind of childish longing and a fetishistic fascination, and I knew that other people did not suffer those disabilities. But in no sense did I feel I was *lying* to the world or to myself. This was simply how things were. I struggle, now, for an analogy that might convey the peculiar pre-closet state, where there is no homosexuality to hide, because everything is hidden. Perhaps I was like the fish in his bowl, seeing everything in the outside world yet utterly apart from it, and unable to conceive of water because to him there is nothing *but* water. A very smart fish might infer that outside of his bowl is something other than water, but he could not really conceive of non-water as being anything but another sort of water. The metaphor of the closet, come to think of it, implies darkness. But the fishbowl is full of light, as much light as in the outside world. I could see everything that everyone else saw. I could touch my lips to a girl's lips, just as other boys did. Yet none of what I saw or did connected to me. It all remained "out there."

I ask myself now: Could I have spoken to someone, in those days? Should I have sought help—as, in fact, Mary suggested? Why did I not? In one sense, the answer is that obviously I needed advice and should have sought it, but did not because I feared being humiliated before my friends and family and I did not want to be diagnosed. Like anyone else, I desired to think of myself as a fundamentally healthy person, and to go to a doctor or—worse—a psychiatrist is to admit that one is "sick." I was prepared to believe that I was abnormal, which one can be in private while getting on with one's life, but not that I was "sick," a state of affairs which makes one's demons a matter of public note and invites—demands!—the intervention of outsiders. Anyone who has been "sick" will tell you that often the hardest part is not the condition itself but the shock to one's identity of presenting oneself to the world as a case for pity and repair. Me, I was bright, successful in school, sociable, a source of pride and hope to my parents. The last thing I wanted was to be a "case."

I say all that, and it is true; but it does not really touch the bottom. For I never got as far as rejecting the possibility of counseling and psychiatric help. What in the world—I would have said then—do I need help *for*? To become somebody else? No. To better accept the way things are? But I accepted things already: I was a freak, and that would either change or I would get used to it. To come to grips, then, with some dark and unspoken, yet suspected, truth about myself? But there was no such unspoken truth! There were, of course, many secrets (starting with Paul), but there was no single Secret. The fishbowl was transparent. It left nothing unseen, nothing dark and "suspected." If I hid my muscle magazines and my overpowering "vicarious admiration" for Paul, that was not because I "suspected" anything about them (as Mary did), but because my kinks were no one else's business. *Of course* I wouldn't discuss them with anyone, any more than I would publicly pull down my pants and waggle a hard-on. The most I ever let myself imagine was that "someday," far off in adulthood, I might "go see someone" to help me work things out.

    I suppose more than a few readers may think it odd that I have said so little about my family and my home. There is a good deal to say about them, some of it perhaps interesting. But all of that, or virtually all of that, is irrelevant to the goings-on I describe here. Today more than ever, we often think of children as a sum of their influences, of their culture and their school and, far above all, their parents. So a memoir must be about the home. But this is not a memoir, exactly; it is an account of a syndrome whose nature was a war with and for a self. Even for a young child, there is such a thing as a sovereign self, something quite apart from the outside world.

I was engaged in a war with that: with an emerging self which I could make no sense of—indeed, which I rejected wholly. My father, who was there, and my mother, who was not, knew nothing of this war. I firmly believe that, great as their influence was in many other departments, in this one it was minimal.

In that single but pervasive respect, a homosexual child, if he is like me, is orphaned. I understood from the beginning that, where all sexual business was concerned, parents were as much a part of the outside world as were, say, the president and Congress. The discovery and development of one's sexuality is virtually synonymous with the discovery and development of a self. It happens inside, and one must deal with it, somehow. That is why no (heterosexual) boy shares his *Playboys* with his parents, and why even the most easygoing of parents are jolted when they realize that their children have erotic lives: here is an entire sector of the child's developing personality which the parent can neither control nor even know. It is as an erotic creature that each of us first comes into his own and achieves separateness. And that is also why one so often hears gay people say their homosexuality is no mere "preference" but a constitutive element of identity: for homosexuals, probably even more than for heterosexuals, it is in the struggle with a burgeoning sexuality that the self discovers it exists.

"A child which appears reasonably happy may actually be

suffering horrors which it cannot or will not reveal," Orwell once said. "It lives in a sort of alien underwater world which we can only penetrate by memory or divination." Yes, that is exactly how it is. Secreting things, clutching mysteries to one's chest, is the essence of childhood. One does not yet fully have a self, and so one does not have a base from which to strike out and seek intimacy with the selves of others. To be a child is to be adrift in a world of riddles and secrets; and in that quite fundamental sense, at least, my childish period lasted long past childhood. It lasted, in fact, until I was 25 years old. Between 15 and 25, I finished high school and went to college and made friends and took jobs and lit out on my own to be a reporter in a strange city. Yet in a curious way, those ten years are blank: lost to love or even the possibility of love. Today they feel, those years, as if they belonged to someone else—as, in a sense, they did. While others were growing up, I was waiting, waiting (but for what?), wide-eyed and dumbstruck and in some measure dead.

6

IN SOME respects, when I look back, the long interval between adolescence and a much-delayed manhood was the most curious of all. Any teenager must gasp and sometimes flee as his sexuality swarms forth in him. From one month to the next, there is no telling how you will feel, or what you may feel impelled to do. The urges buck and rear and stomp, and you balance precariously atop, fighting for nothing more glorious than to stay off the ground. By eighteen or nineteen, the bucking and pitching have slowed, and you are more or less as you will be, and so, if you are not an invert, you turn your attention to earning your spurs. On the other hand, if you are an invert, you—or I, in any case—move from a turmoil of luridly blooming abnormality to an eerie twilit stasis. Your erotic being becomes like an elephant in the living room, to be left alone if possible, or to be humored when it stirs and threatens to upset furniture, but in any case not to be frontally grappled with. The important thing is to avoid wondering precisely *why* there is an elephant in your living room, which you can do by assuming that everyone has an elephant in the house; or by feeling assured that the thing is not after all an elephant but a large, irregularly shaped divan; or by supposing that tomorrow the elephant will be gone as mysteriously as it came; or simply by mentally changing the subject—or, indeed, by doing all of the above, as I did. I was like the lawyer who tells the judge that his client did not steal the car, that the car was worthless and didn't work anyway, and in any case the client returned the car in perfect condition. The casualty, of course, was love, which was submerged under the weight of preconscious or half-conscious denial. But at least—an ugly sort of blessing, this—the denial became less like the frenzy of the man whirling to put out fires all over his body and more like the steady ache of a man with a burn. The main thing, on which all else depended, was not to stir up the elephant.

On the other hand, those very first years of male adulthood are not a good time to be a eunuch. This is when young men realize they are beautiful and begin to exercise the magnetism of their newly minted manhood. The very first sight which met me when I moved into my college dorm was Dean Carrigan, lolling in the entryway with his shirt conspicuously absent. I am sure I was not the only one who noticed that his chest and shoulders had been molded by three or four years in the gym. With all the not-quite-innocence of a young man's narcissism, he once let me try to put both of my hands around his arms while I wondered aloud how he had grown them. In one of my first college classes, I found myself sitting next to Dan Grissom, a gymnast who was partial to T-shirts. Everywhere, now, on all sides, around every corner, there were more and more of these men—not boys now!—who exuded what I called simply "It," meaning, I think, mature masculinity with a hint of flaunted sexiness. The "envy," the rage, continued. I began to notice the thoroughbred masculinity of athletic men's buttocks. Or, to be more accurate, my eyes and head and loins began to notice, for "I" resolutely didn't. My head would swivel right around when an upperclassman passed by in a flattering pair of jeans, or when a jock pounded past in jogging shorts. Fortunately, I understood why my head involuntarily turned like an owl's: I *envied* the way these men looked in their clothes and wanted to learn just how they accomplished it. No doubt there was a trick to finding pants that fit so well, and by studying the matter I might figure it out.

More and more, I just let my head turn. I mean, why not? I could not imagine why I was neurotically obsessed with the cut of men's Levi's as seen from the rear, and I knew the swiveling head was strange, if not actually demented, but it didn't seem to do me any harm. During the semester, I would watch the parade of cocky masculinity flow by on all sides. During the summer, there was still Paul.

He had changed, too. By now I had grown an inch or more taller than he, so I looked down at him instead of up. But the precociously muscled high-school boy was now a broad, brick-hard man with four years of lifting weights under his belt, or, more aptly, under his shirt. By this time I had worked up the nerve to lift weights myself a little— to no apparent effect—and whenever I could, I went down to the gym with Paul and let myself float in the hot tingle as he stripped off his T-shirt after a workout and we critically appraised his sweaty chest. Now, though, I was a bit older and not quite as desperately crazy with hormones, and so I was less vampiric and goggle-eyed in my attentions; he also was a bit older, and had become used to getting some attention for his body, and didn't mind getting a bit more. He became, to me, something more like a human being, and less like a god. I became, to him, a friend with whom he could share his hobby. I was still overwhelmed by him, crushed in the Jovian gravitational field emanating from his body; I still thrilled to the sight of him and sang myself to sleep three nights out of four by conjuring images of him. But this, too, attained a kind of perverse normalcy, a stasis. I began to feel like a man who finds that his disease has stopped progressing, and who begins to see that he can cope with his infirmities. So this, I thought, will be my life. This is what I must get used to: a head which swivels of its own accord, a body which is without any proper sexual impulse, and a flash flood of "envy" and frustration when I am confronted with certain men. So be it. A dull blackness set in.

I felt nothing for women, sexually. I would have been grateful for even the slightest arousal, which I still half-expected any day, but there was nothing, not anything. Sometimes women would take an interest in me, but my unresponsiveness quickly sent them away. I was not cold or discouraging, but rather more (or less) than that: I was childlike, responding with no response at all except to change the subject. On only two occasions did I try anything with a woman. The first was when I was 20. I was sitting with two of my friends in a college courtyard one day when somehow we met a girl named, I think, Judy. She was only seventeen or eighteen but already a sophomore, and she had, she let us know, been around with older men. Not only that: *German* men. The conversation became a little more explicit, and pretty soon we began to gather that she might be interested in one or more of us. And that evening she called me. So one night soon after, I ushered her into my dorm room and closed the shutters. She smoked; we talked; I waited for something to happen, supposing that something *would* happen and desperately hoping I would make a go of it. For a change, I felt grown up. An assignation! (With a smoker!) Finally, when she got tired of waiting, she said, "So. Aren't you going to take your clothes off?" Gulping, I did, as matter-of-factly as if in the fitting room at Macy's, though I kept my undershorts on. She drew back and took me in, head to toe, and said, "God. Your legs look like you just escaped from Auschwitz."

I am happy to report that even then, at that memorable moment, I understood that this was funny. Not because she was kidding (she wasn't), but because the whole situation was absurd. An asexual man-boy tries sex for the first time at a moment of existential vulnerability and she says—*what*? I could hear the cosmos chortling, though I was not myself in a laughing mood. After that, you can imagine, a whole different sort of half-heartedness was added to my list of problems that night. I was not aroused, not even close. There was some pointless rubbing. She left. I, to my own surprise, had little trouble putting the whole incident aside. Mercifully, her comment had given me just cause to fail. Whatever my assignation had been, it was neither sex nor romance nor even affectionate exploration, I understood. It was irrelevant. And so I shrugged and took it in stride.

The second time was different. By my last year in college, I had become close friends with Elissa, a tall, sharp-minded, good-natured woman in the junior class. We became intimates, saw some movies together, took some meals together. I went home with her for a holiday and met her mother, who took a shine to me. (Parents often seem to like their children's homosexual friends: so well-mannered.) It was logical for me to wonder whether we were in fact dating, even though I felt nothing more than friendly feelings for her. She wondered too. A night came in March when we were talking together in her dorm room and it was late and there was no one around. One of us (me?) wondered if maybe I should be with her that night. She was willing. I was eager. Not, I mean, *sexually* eager: hardly that! I knew, however, that if my mature sexuality was ever going to arrive, this was the moment. It had to be now. I was alone with a girl I liked, and she wanted me. All the ingredients were there to flip the switch. The only thing I needed to do was tell her my awful sexual secret, since it seemed imprudent not to give her fair warning that the flight might be a choppy one. This was something that I had never said to anybody, although I knew full well that plenty of people suspected it. So, mustering my nerve, I swallowed hard and told her the truth. "I'm a virgin," I confessed. She knew. She knew, she didn't mind, she was not much more experienced, she expected no virtuosity. It was perfect.

I rushed down to my room, found a condom, roared back upstairs, took off some clothes, turned off some lights, dived into bed. It occurred to me, about then, that I had no idea what to do. I mean not that I had *no* idea. I had seen a few magazines and the odd movie or two, so I had an approximate mental image of where I was supposed to wind up and what I was meant to be doing there. What I lacked, however, was any clear plan for getting into that position.

For nothing was happening. I might as well have been in bed with a walrus. I no longer remember what I tried or what she tried. We both gave up after less than an hour and just lay there. I remember being naked and feeling humiliated, sunk; I remember eventually putting my underpants back on; I remember her professing not to mind. I crept back to my room the next morning, after a night of little sleep in a narrow dormitory bed, the unopened condom still in my pocket and no joyful smirk on my face.

After that I never tried again with her or any other woman. For a week, I sank into a depression such as I have never known since, for my failure, not only to get aroused but to feel any guiding spark of eros, could mean only one thing. I now was forced to confront a truth about myself I had hoped never to have to face. I was impotent.

"Don't be silly," my mother said on the telephone. In the depression I felt after my second sexual fiasco, I opened the door a crack and reached out just enough to tell her I had been unable to get it up with a girl. "You're not impotent. The body doesn't lie, that's all. Sometimes you're not in the mood. Sometimes you're nervous. It happens to everybody." Yes, but I knew the truth: I had never experienced "the mood," and now I knew I could not simulate it. Truly, I had no sexuality, no masculinity. I did not even have a functional penis. My last hope had been that when the time came my body would know what to do and lead me, at last, to my missing sexuality. Now I looked ahead and saw two ghoulish lives beckoning. In one, I kept trying sex, kept failing, kept swallowing my humiliation until perhaps at last the plumbing worked or I gave up. In the other life, I was too cowardly even to try, and I accommodated myself to an existence as the planet's only wholly asexual person.

I did the only sensible thing, under the circumstances. I waited for the depression to clear, and then went back to thinking about it all as little as I could. Of course, one has to think of such a matter a good deal, especially in one's early twenties, when eros is as thick in the air among males as pollen in verdant spring. Others were talking about their girlfriends or lack of them; I had nothing to say. Looking back, that, at least, is a point of pride, if only a sad and tenuous one. When a young man, at the age of 21, looks inside himself and sees only an alien fascination, sees just a weird obsession with muscles and well-fitting blue jeans rather than any proper sort of hunger for love—such a young man can no longer be said, at his age, merely to be a boy, a larva. He is, rather, pithed, all busyness but no soul, a non-man. It was not that I had failed to fall in love: sexual love, as I understood it, the passionate hungry embrace of another, seemed not just unattainable but inconceivable. I was not so much unhappy as in a sort of limbo, a region without proper sexual topography of any kind, but with bizarre undercurrents and caves and lava eruptions everywhere underfoot. The worst thing about my limbo, I think, was not the emptiness—one could get used to that, and in any case one kept oneself busy—but the absence of a proper self, of the sovereign heart that loves and may be loved. At that place, in the core, there seemed only echoing gibberish and gaseous fumes.

The great problem for a self-less man is the difficulty of any sort of integrity. "This above all, to thine own self be true." But what is the self-less man to be true *to*? Not his beloved, for he recognizes no beloved. Not his heart, for his heart is in cold storage. Not, certainly, his sexuality, for he does not imagine himself to have a sexuality. Not his personality, for at the core of his personality is a raging obsession which he views as less an element of self than as a kind of fungus. Perhaps, then, at least to his feelings, such as they are? But those he cannot face. He can live with them, but not assimilate them. They are in him but not of him, like a herpes strain.

I found, in the end, only one way to assert some sense of integrity, and so of selfhood: I did not lie. Groups of us talked about girls (later, women). In college, my friends would sit in a group in a dormitory courtyard and lecherously peer up at windows in hopes of catching some girl making love, or would sing the praises of someone's breasts. But I never joined in. On all such occasions I simply went mute. I never pretended to be interested in *Penthouse*, never eulogized any part of any woman, never invented sexual exploits or even sexual fantasies. I just sat. This was my one and only act of self-assertion, of defiance; and I think now that it was a rather brave one, given that lying in these matters is not only common among young men but expected. If I was a eunuch, then by God I would pretend to be nothing else. In that way, at least, I found it possible to have a fragment of dignity.

7

AS I DID NOT speak to others, so I did not speak to myself. The stimulation of love, so important in those years of early adulthood, was replaced by a numb routine of loveless fantasy and mechanical stimulation. Instead of dating and hope and heartbreak, there was only the image of Paul, brought forth as needed and then put away again, like a page from a dirty magazine. There was the "envy," of course, that constant disruptive companion. That was all. I walked forward on a treadmill, in motion but moving nowhere, keeping my eyes pointed downward on the ground, straight ahead. There was only today, no tomorrow, because life could not go on forever in this way, but there was no prospect of anything else. Thus did months stretch into years as I gradually gave up on becoming a fully formed human being. How odd it now seems that I was mostly cheerful rather than miserable; but people adapt to stranger conditions.

DENIAL

Only occasionally, in all those years, did hints of a different world flash through chinks in the wall. When I was eighteen, I found myself spending the night in a friend's dorm room, and there in the sanctuary of the dark he told me what he said he had never confided before: that he often had sexual fantasies about the hair on men's arms and legs. The relief I felt upon telling him—as I had told no one—about my, um, interest in muscles was nothing compared with my relief, and astonishment, upon learning that another outwardly normal boy was baffled by a bizarre sexual, or pseudosexual, or asexual, obsession. Hair: that was even stranger than biceps! This was the first intimation that I was not the only monster: I might at least be a monster of a recurrent type.

Later that year, an aging college professor (who taught Greek classics, no less) fell deeply in love with me. I rejected his advances but accepted his friendship, until the two became awkwardly inseparable, and then I left his orbit. Though he was kind to me and taught me much—explained wines, expounded on platonic love, took me to the opera, told me of Agra and Bangkok and Athens—he was a rotund bald man with bad yellow teeth, and his lonely weekend trips to haunt gay bars and strip joints in Manhattan struck me as sad and seedy. If this was a homosexual, I could hardly be one. On the other hand, I knew that his obsession with my beauty, as he saw it, was no fabrication. I could see the way my presence affected his eyes and his face; I could see the flush in his cheeks and the hunger in his gaze. His lust frightened me but also fascinated me. I was flattered, but more than that: so intense was his desire for me that it pierced, briefly, my self-loathing. No, I was not *really* beautiful—of course not! But I could exert the power of beauty at least over one aging, sad homosexual. I could make him feel as helpless and stricken as I always felt.

In the gay parlance, people who exert beauty over others and who know that they do so are said to have "attitude," and are often envied and resented. Certainly the resentment is understandable. The first really crushing sense of powerlessness I knew, apart from the powerlessness of childhood itself, was when I realized, as a schoolboy, that any boy in my class could overpower me in a fight, render me helpless and make me subject to his whim. Oddly, this realization was accompanied not just with consternation but also titillation. Domination is sexy. Hollywood knows that watching a man being kicked in the face and forced to submit delivers an erotic charge to males; boys know it, too. I gradually found my own kinds of strength, but then I was flattened all over again. This time it was another kind of powerlessness that crushed me. In the presence of Paul, I felt as a dog must when it lies on its back and waves its paws in surrender. At such a time, one knows that only submission and inferiority are possible, and that one can only play one's role and try to escape with one's dignity. For all men, I think, the desire to dominate is never wholly subdued, however civilization may (or may not) mask it. Although economic and political power are heady, aesthetic power—the power of the inspired preacher or singer or film maker or writer—is at least as intoxicating. I write for many reasons, but none is more important than the impulse to exert beauty over others. It is, in a petty way, vengeance for the humiliation of having been enslaved by beauty myself. But the power of a beautiful contrivance is nothing next to the power of the object of lust. For the first time, I—of all people!—held the slave master's chain.

I made no bones about what seemed to me to be the professor's folly. Again and again I told him the truth: that I was the skinniest, geekiest eighteen-year-old in the world. I felt, in the face of his love, like the honest man who is offered a million dollars for a lump of coal by people who believe it to be a rare gem. No, no, I said, you have the wrong man, you should direct your desire where it belongs. I pointed out—truth in advertising—that I was pale, bowlegged, humpbacked, pimply, gawky, physically immature. He parried all my protests. Ah, he would cry, how could I be so wrong? Did I not know I had smooth white skin, gracefully youthful lines, lithe muscles, deep brown eyes, and a keen intelligence which made all the rest glow? Did I not understand that in the age of the Greeks, I would have been a prize sought by many an older man? Preposterous, I thought. Yet I knew he was sincere and that somehow I had been given a magic hold over him. And so for a few months I entered into a friendship, in which he adored and instructed me and I relished his company and, frankly, his servitude.

Over Thanksgiving break, when I planned to stay on campus rather than make the long trek back to Phoenix, I had nothing to do, and so one day I appeared at my professor friend's door with a suggestion. Why don't you take me to New York for a few days, and show me around? He had mentioned to me, earlier, that he could show me both the highest and lowest of New York City's culture, and the idea tantalized and titillated me. An adventure with a professor! Receiving my proposition, he flushed, perhaps realizing (as I naïvely did not) that I was putting both of us in a compromising situation, and said he would do it only if I got my father's approval. No problem there, and so in a few weeks I found myself staying with him in a shabby-genteel hotel room just off Times Square, conveniently close to the Gaiety Theater, a gay strip club where the dancers were available for carry-out, at a price. He kept his word and showed me both sides of the city. We heard Jon Vickers sing at the Metropolitan Opera, saw *The Gin Game* on Broadway, and toured the Metropolitan Museum and the Museum of Modern Art and the Frick Collection. Also, he brought me to the Gaiety, where I felt sorry for the boys on the stage and sorry for the professor who craved them and sorry for the shadowy figures

DENIAL

around us who I suspected were masturbating in the dark.

Afterward, the professor took me to his favorite bar: not a loud dance club but a dim watering hole behind an unmarked door. He insisted on having a glass of wine or two, or three, before bed—the better, I suspected, to work up his nerve to seduce me, and so I sat nearby, determinedly sober, on my guard. Perched on a stool, bundled tortoise-like under a puffy down jacket and a woolen watch cap, with my back defensively to the wall, I passed the time nervously watching as the hookers worked the pool tables in the back of the room. And then the door opened and in walked...oh, *no*! To this day I remember how, as the man entered the bar, his eyes swept the room. No flash of recognition crossed his visage as he made his way past me and on toward the pool tables to arrange his evening's entertainment, but as soon as the coast was clear, I dashed to the bar and told the professor we had to leave, *now*. Couldn't he finish his wine? *NOW.* Why? (he said)—what's the problem? The man (I replied) who just walked in: *he's my uncle.*

I had heard from my mother, who despised her younger brother, that he was gay. I barely knew him, but—just my luck!—I had paid him a visit only a few weeks before, and so my face would be fresh in his mind. What if he had spotted me? The professor spent the next two hours walking me around the streets of New York, talking me down from my panic. I was not in trouble, I was not now a known homosexual, my uncle probably had not recognized me, and if he had recognized me, he would not rat me out and indeed he would be more worried that I might rat *him* out. Eventually I stopped shaking, but still: it had been an unnervingly close call. That night was my last peek into the gay underworld for years. What little adventurousness I had mustered evaporated. Even to explore, I realized, was too risky.

Once I calmed down, the professor, as I might have expected, propositioned me, pleading for sex in our hotel room; to his credit, he took no for an answer. It turned out I had been right to trust him. At the end of the semester, he moved away for a job in Boston, and I knew that this was just as well, a convenient way to end what had inevitably become an awkward friendship, inasmuch as he loved me desperately and I would do no more than shake his hand. Also, in New York, at the Gaiety and in the bar and in the dingy hotel room, I had seen his sadness and isolation. He was the very picture of the lonely, squalid homosexual: everything I knew, or prayed, I was not. It was time to be rid of him. He asked, however, for a parting gift: a pair of my undershorts and a chance to see me pose in them before I gave them to him, unwashed. His request struck me as pitiable; my own fantasies in which Paul posed and flexed his sweaty muscles while I trembled at his feet did not seem in any way comparable. Still, one cold night in December, I walked to his apartment with a grocery bag under my arm, and I gave him his gift, standing on an ottoman in his bedroom after making sure he had shut the blinds and turned up the heat. I did it out of vanity and pity, if those were not in fact the same. Vanity, so as to feel my power over him, so as to watch his cheeks grow pink and his forehead moist as I did nothing more than stand before and over him. Pity, because I knew so well—and, all that time, so secretly—what it was to gulp and tremble and feel the guts jump nearly out of the skin at the sight of a superhuman other. Years later, when, as an openly gay man, I saw him again, he told me he would always remember my kindness to him that Christmas. But I did not feel very generous.

When the episode with him was over, everything was the same as before. He was kind and ugly and pitiable, I was sweet and ugly and pitiable. Our lives had crossed and then gone straight on, separately. He confirmed for me that I was no homosexual, because I felt no longing at all for the soft white skin of boys still a step or two from full manhood; indeed, I was repulsed by the idea. Whatever I felt had nothing to do with boys and smoothness and prettiness; it had to do with men and hardness, with muscle and beard. I would go on, after I met him, for another seven years adrift on my slate-gray, mirror-smooth sea of sexlessness. When I left the university, I took a job as a newspaper reporter in a southern town, where I made several gay friends but never broached any subject smacking of love or desire—for I felt no love or desire, only the unending enslavement to Paul and the "envy" that accompanied every step I took. I had grown used to my eunuchhood: it was my natural condition. Nothing had changed, nothing would change.

This was not a painful time, when I left school and set out as what they used to call a cub reporter. Rather it was a time of eerie calm, like a suspension in motionlessness while I nonetheless moved at a frantic pace. I recall those final two years or so of inversion as an energetic trance, a Saint Vitus's dance which I performed in my sleep. At the newspaper, I was assigned to a surly but able assistant city editor, a grumpy taskmaster straight from central casting who had little use for Ivy League boys and kept me hopping. I covered a tornado, a fatal fire, an arrest for illegal cockfighting, a university scandal, a total eclipse, an entertaining school board. I reviewed local concerts and plays, I collected rejection slips from famous publications. I had plenty to do. Odd things would sometimes happen to me, too. One day, driving along North University Boulevard, I rear-ended a delivery van. It seems I had taken my eyes off the road to take a long gander at a young man in a nearby pickup truck. As usual, my head had swiveled of its own accord, drawn by an invisible magnet. I recall thinking, as I later paid for the van's new taillight, that I really must get this peculiar habit under control, because it could cause me some trouble. Otherwise, I put the incident out of my mind. By now I had grown used to knowing that I was the strangest creature in the world, one whose wiring was seemingly random. My body had filled out and my teenager's exaggerated sensitivity had begun to wane, so, although I knew I was ugly, I realized that I was less ugly than before, and I cared less. My outings to the weight room were beginning to make a difference. So I was less inclined to explain my erotic tics and upwellings, my head-turnings and my palpitations in the presence of leonine Daryl who lived down the street, as manifestations of "envy." I became less inclined to explain them at all. I began to give up trying to understand, which I suppose was in itself a step toward acceptance. Where, as a teenager, I had writhed and wrestled for a way out until my joints were twisted and my skin raw, by 23 I had begun to feel resigned. An empty mind was better than a crazy one, and there were some things about myself which I was fated not to comprehend and which I thus had better not think about.

It was this blanking-out of all loving outreach and, more, of all thoughts of loving outreach which gave those years of my early twenties the feeling of a wakeful coma. I carefully avoided being caught where I might be in danger of intimacy with a woman. There were no dates for me, and few unchaperoned encounters. All my friends were men, and with them I was careful never to talk about sex or romance. I was aware that they were exploring and settling whole emotional continents where I had never set foot, and that they were busy seeking and embracing love while I was busy shunning it. *Oh, well, to each his own,* I thought—*some people are "into" love and sex, and some people aren't, and I'm one of the aren'ts.* Of course, I had no sex life. I had heard of West Fourth Street, where at night gay men cruised slowly past each other in their cars, but I had no inclination to go there. For a time, I managed to make myself respond erotically to pictures of women bodybuilders, mainly by imagining they were men. Mostly, however, I simply turned off the lights in the central section of my personality and moved out, occupying only the side rooms and the outbuildings. I was more numb than unhappy. I lived in the half-light preceding a dawn which never comes. And at night, to lull me to sleep, there was still—still, ten years later—the comfort of Paul, now 2,000 miles away, yet still flexing and preening and performing feats of strength there in my dim bedroom, just for me.

I say things were "mostly" like that, because there were breakdowns. Vacating the center of one's own personality, living without a soul, is not such an easy thing to do, even if one tries very hard. Unpredictably, stimulated by a sight or a sound or a stray thought, the covering which I had tacked over my vacant center would sometimes blow aside. Sometimes I had panic attacks, so intense and enveloping that I remember them with specificity to this day. One night I was watching *Risky Business*, a coming-of-age story in which a teenager loses his virginity to a beautiful young prostitute while his parents are out of town. At some point during the movie, as the boy crossed to manhood by having sex with a beautiful woman, I noticed a flare of anxiety ignite in the pit of my stomach, and then, as I wondered what was going on, it spread until I was full of a fear which I could not at first identify. The panic reached my brain and the fear assumed a shape, which was foreknowledge of a future in which nothing begat nothing and the loving touch of another would never come. My initiation into the world of love should have happened years earlier but had not happened and could not happen and never would happen and there, suddenly, was the mouth of the void roaring wide before me and the chill wind cutting through me, and the void, the blackness, was my heart. The movie fragmented into unintelligibility, and the chair under me disappeared. I tumbled and reeled for a while and then forced my mind to push outward, back to the movie, back to rational cognition. Yes, I was a sad case (I told myself), yes, it was unusual to be a virgin at my age, yes, it was even more unusual to avoid all opportunities to "get some experience." But calm down, calm down, the time will come, this cannot go on forever, it cannot, others must have been here, and surely they found their way out eventually, *eventually*. After a time, the panic subsided, though it was followed by an unease which lasted longer. Then the numbness mercifully returned.

I now recall only one or two occasions when I had any

inkling that the walls and pillars of my weird prison might in fact be unsteady, that something was stirring which would change everything. One such occasion was when I clipped a jeans advertisement that showed, not a freakish muscleman (or musclewoman), but a handsome young model with a hint of an inviting smile. I tore him out and put him in my shirt pocket, savoring the feeling that in some way (how?) I was playing with matches. Not long after, when I switched jobs and cities, I noticed a gym ad showing a group of men who looked decidedly ... gay. With the same feeling of titillation and mischief, I clipped that ad and decided that maybe it would be *this* gym that I would join. Why not? What harm could it do? Probably, I thought, the people there would be friendly.

Those were more or less the only hints. In a classic experiment of cognitive psychology, subjects were asked to wear goggles that made them see everything upside-down. For a time, the wearer is at a loss, confused, almost distraught; but then, after a period of adjustment, there is a sudden change. One morning the subject awakens to find—voilà!—that the world is righted again. He is aware of no process of mental correction, no intermediate period when the world is tilted at 45 degrees, then 90. The transformation is sudden and total (and the same is true in reverse, after the goggles come off). During my long period as an invert, I was unaware of my inversion; I was also unaware of any movement away from it. But then the time came to lie once again, and it was one lie too many. And suddenly, gasping, shocked, mortified, thrilled, I was flat on the ground looking at a world which, for the first time, made sense.

8

IT IS VERY difficult for an ordinary heterosexual to imagine that an ordinary homosexual is in fact not, deep inside, a repressed heterosexual who needs to try harder with women or just get his act together. However, the effect of women on me was always to reinforce my erotic alienation from them. Encountering them was like searching through a tank of octopuses in hopes of finding one to marry. Mostly I stopped trying, but I still hoped that one day a woman would come along who did not, erotically speaking, have eight tentacles with suckers on them. Miss Right might yet solve my problem!

I met Maxine (not, as they say, her real name, but I have always wanted to write about a woman named Maxine) six months before my 25th birthday. Our sisters set us up, and it was clear from the first few minutes that this could work. We were both journalists, both the same age. She had a warm, empathetic, unpretentious personality and a mind which seemed to anticipate my own thoughts; she took herself seriously but was never solemn; she worked too hard and had as much confidence as a 24-year-old is entitled to, but with a girlish vulnerability which made me feel, amazing to say it, masculine. Whether one likes this or that person is less important, finally, than whether one likes oneself *with* this or that person. I liked myself with Maxine, and she, I think, liked herself with me. She was one of those people whom it is difficult to think ill of. We quickly fell deeply in like.

For a few months, we would go to movies together, then have a late dinner and gab at each other across the table. Then I would take her home—she lived a mile away from me—and leave her at the door, or, after a while, come inside for a bit. And I would peck her on the cheek, birdlike, and go home, trilling goodnight as I left. Thanks—lovely evening—let's do it again soon—bye!

At some point, sitting there next to her on her sofa at half past eleven, I must have been struck by the thought that something more was expected from me than conversation. But I knew where "something more" might lead, and so I preferred to overlook this detail. We were friends, we might someday become more than friends, what was wrong with that? And so I kept the conversation burbling amiably about our jobs, our bosses, our hometowns, our sisters, whatever. All the while, I made good and sure to be on the opposite end of the sofa, with my hands safely out of harm's way. I did not kiss her; I did not touch her. Apparently, as women sometimes do, she noticed.

Her manner, after a time, began to evince puzzlement and frustration. I sensed it, and a common friend of ours confirmed it. He was gay, and he wordlessly but all too clearly believed that I might be a member of the club. I was annoyed by his insinuations, but they did at last help force the issue. In high school, with Mary, I had waited until she broke off. In college, with Elissa, I had panicked. After Elissa, I gave up and made myself too busy to think about it. Never had I faced a woman squarely and confessed to being incapable of love. What young man could confess such a thing? But this time, for the first time, I had an idea that I was not a eunuch after all. One day, soon after I first met Maxine, I heard myself talking quietly, tentatively, with a gay man who had become a close friend. I told him what I had never told anyone: I told him of my strange fixation on Paul, on his muscles and hands and skin. And then I heard myself ask, using carefully ungendered pronouns: If I want desperately to see a person with their shirt off and can't not think about them—could that be some sort of … crush? Some kind of *love*? And there was a pause before, ever so tenderly, he smiled and said, "Jonathan, it sure sounds that way to me."

Love! That horrible burning thrill, that possessing obsession, that sense of physiological enthrallment to another—had I felt it after all? All along, for ten years or more, had I been hopelessly infatuated? Well ... possibly.

There was no effect of scales tumbling from my eyes that night, no noticeable change in my life or my behavior. There was only an idea with many implications, none of which I was ready, at that moment, to consider. But Maxine made further delay impossible. I sensed her exasperation and self-doubt and realized that I must talk to her, say something, or risk hurting her. To my credit—this is something I am proud of to the present day—my integrity asserted itself. Whatever else happened, I would not lie. I would not suffer *that* humiliation. One night we went out for dinner. We chatted in the usual way, and I briefly imagined that I might yet squirm off the hook. No. After dinner we went for a walk. It was a cool April night with the sweetness of an earlier rainfall still in the air, and we must have circled the block five times. She wanted to know, she said, where she stood. I hemmed and hawed. Gently, implacably, she said nothing, demanding, with her silence, a reply. It took me many minutes of gulping and croaking to tell her what I suspected. I told her I thought I might be gay and said I would look for professional help.

That was a few days before my 25th birthday. It was some time before I found my feet in a new world. At first I had dreams of a whole new sort, like someone else's dreams. I dreamed about being homosexually raped. In one dream I was driving with a gay man whose friendship I felt honored to have, but we were crossing a desert alone and he turned to me and said, "You know what has to happen." In another dream I was groped by several men in a locker room, and though I resisted, I wasn't sure I disliked what was happening. There was an afternoon—not a dream, now—when I was sweeping my kitchen floor and was all at once overwhelmed, flattened, by a thought that welled up to swamp the broom and the kitchen and everything. *Oh God, oh God, I don't want to be a homosexual!* For is the homosexual not an outsider, alone? (Bad enough to be a Jew!) But the fear, real as it was, was succeeded by relief. I had wanted above all else not to be monstrous, to be capable of love, to have an adult self. A homosexual is unusual, yes, and in some important ways disadvantaged: notably, in the inability to conceive and raise biological children with his beloved. Unlike some homosexuals, I do not feel it to be self-hating or demeaning to say that I, at least, feel homosexuality as a (mild) disability: not crippling, not in any way a moral infirmity, but I feel that there is a grand mystery in life to which I will never be privy. However, many people, probably more of them straight than gay, accommodate themselves happily to that (mild) disability. Some adopt, some go with sperm banks and surrogates, and some have books instead of babies. I had resisted imagining myself as a homosexual, or even imagining that it might be possible for me to be a homosexual, because I had supposed that to be a homosexual is to lose any possibility of a normal life. Then Maxine nudged me across the line, and what I could never have imagined before was suddenly the very nose on my face: only within the context of homosexuality—of a frank acknowledgment that I love men and want to be loved by men—was normalcy possible for me. For all those dreary years, I had made myself a monster in my desperation not to be one.

A year passed before I "did" anything about my discovery, and longer before I became comfortable writing and talking and thinking about it. Months passed before I told my family (I wanted to be sure). I never did recover from the loss of my adolescence; I never completely filled the vacuum where my awakening to love and sexuality and self ought to have been. But in some respects, change came so fast that it can barely be described as change at all. What came was less a change than a differentness, sudden and total. In that respect, it was quite like the adjustment to the upside-down spectacles. Or, if you like, imagine being born and raised in a dark dungeon cell, where you hear of an outside world but cannot conceive of a path to it; and then imagine that one day you put your fingers to the brick and push a bit, just the slightest bit of pressure, and all four walls of the cell simply collapse into the ground, and all traces of captivity are gone except the ones inscribed on yourself. Before, nothing had made sense except with the most contorted applications of pseudo-logic; now the sense in things was obvious. I knew, now, what the "envy" was.

And, behold, now it was not envy at all. It was lust: red-blooded, vigorous, primate lust, joyous and pounding with life. Explain it away? To the contrary! Like a parched man finding a river, I drank it in and reveled in it. The fetish for muscular men, for strength and athleticism? One day after my confession to Maxine, I hesitantly told a gay friend that, well, I know this sounds weird, but, um, I kind of have an obsession with muscular men. Let me just say that he was not exactly shocked, except maybe by my naïveté. "Don't we all?" he said, with a smile and a sigh. *Don't we all*? What I did not say to him, but longed to cry out, was that for me, from my first days of consciousness until the day before yesterday, there was no "we," there was no "all," only the all-confining and unique me, the universe of one. And now suddenly what had been bizarre was commonplace, even trite. Overnight I had gone from monster to cliché.

Now I knew why my head swiveled when I passed a handsome man on the street: why I had rear-ended that van on North University Boulevard. Now I knew why I was so interested in men's blue jeans—when, that is, they were on men's bottoms. Now I knew why in high school I thrilled to every glimpse of Paul's big muscles and adoringly catalogued his feats of strength. Though I would not wish upon my worst enemy the time I spent in gray limbo, there was, I suppose, some compensation in the miraculous experience of being born anew into a world of color. For a time, every day or two seemed to bring some new revelation. One day I told a gay friend that I had always wanted to be big and muscular, and he replied, without missing a beat, "No, that's who you want to *marry*." For him this was a casual witticism, but for me it had the force of newly minted truth. I did not need to *be* one of these men I had stared at for so long with hopeless "envy." What I needed to do was love one.

How can I describe to you what it was like to be awakened to the ability to love? It was rehabilitating, it was redeeming: not the state of love (or of lust), but the possibility of love. I abhor some of what Catholicism teaches about homosexuality, but I appreciate that in one respect the Church has come to see us whole. Where it used to regard homosexuality as a mere behavior, engaged in sinfully by heterosexuals, it now understands that some men love men and some women love women, and are so constituted as to have no meaningful choice in the matter. Where many denominations regard same-sex love itself as wicked, the Catholic Church asks of homosexuals not that they be heterosexual but that they remain celibate, which is, at least, possible. Now, to ask a human being to dwell in a bed of solitude without the touch of another, until God Himself extends His embrace, is to ask for the most profound and, for most people, enormous of sacrifices. Many people would rather die in loving company than live alone. That, indeed, is what makes the priestly vow of celibacy the supreme act of devotion that it is. There surely are some people who can live whole and healthy lives without sex. I know a middle-aged Catholic woman who, because she is both unmarried and devout, is celibate by choice. She is vibrant and proud, partly, of course, because her celibacy is chosen and principled, rather than furtive or paralytic. But to be celibate is one thing; to live without even the possibility of love is something else again, a stripping-out of self and soul which leaves behind an ageless child.

In truth, I now have trouble myself remembering how the world looked on the other side, through the upside-down goggles. I less remember that past than reconstruct it. Sometimes, like a man who has gained sight after a lifetime of blindness, I wonder whether people who grew up with a normal experience of love really appreciate what they have. Sometimes, too, I reflect that if people could be shorn, for only a week, of the capacity for love they might understand the scalding cruelty of maintaining that homosexuals cannot, or should not, decently love. What homosexuals, what all humans, cannot decently do is deny love.

9

"**T**HUS I BEGAN my new life," said David Copperfield, "with everything new about me." And thus I also began mine, a life of success and failure and pleasure and irritation and love and loss, unlike any other man's life but also like all of them: in short, the life, at long last, of a man, rather than of a stunted child. David Copperfield reflected that a curtain had fallen forever on his old, wretched life, and he "lifted it for a moment, even in this narrative, with a reluctant hand, and dropped it gladly." I have lifted the curtain from a remove which allows curiosity and even some affectionate remembrance rather than horror, but I share with David Copperfield a shuddering gratitude that it is all, now, over. Of course, all children and teenagers, and many adults too, have their secret nightmares to live through: but to some extent mine was set apart from many others', first, by its imperviousness not only to outside influences but to my own exertions to escape it, and, second, by its long occupation and sudden, transformative decampment. Many people, especially young people, struggle against many infirmities of the soul and anguishes of the heart, but I did not so much struggle against mine as writhe within it, and then in the end I did not so much overcome it as simply release it, and then watch as it burst like a soap bubble into thin air. Such, perhaps, is the nature of an inversion: impregnable and excruciating when viewed from within, but feeble and silly when seen from without.

What is especially difficult for me to understand now about my lost world on the other side of the moon is how I could have thrashed so hard to construct "sensible" explanations for the crazy state of things, yet never have seen the countless glaring contradictions in the account of things on which I settled. How could I have been certain that I had no interest in touching a man when my pulse doubled every time I brushed against Paul? How could I have read and heard about teenage crushes and yet conclude that I had never felt one? Why, why in the world, would *envy* give me an erection? How was I able to suppose that my feelings, so obviously and hydraulically sexual in their effect, had nothing to do with sexuality? The sheer epic perverseness of it now strikes me as amazing. The baroque tortuous confusion and the twisting of the self—what an extraordinary business!

Above all, I now wonder, why was I so much more

willing to believe that I was a monster than a homosexual? Why was I prepared to be a deformed and loveless heterosexual rather than a queer? I knew full well, then, that my parents were not the sort who would reject or torment a homosexual child. My mother lived in sandaled, beaded Berkeley, where many of her male friends were gay. When I finally told her I was gay, she all but yawned. It is true that my own Phoenix, Arizona, was far from Berkeley in every sense, a conservative place; but it was more Goldwater conservative than Falwell conservative, and in any case I rejected hostility toward homosexuals as bigotry, and indeed wore this rejection as a badge of my decency. I did not hate homosexuality in others, so why would I hate it in myself?

To some extent, I conclude, my inversion was born of naïveté. I had little idea what a homosexual was, and when it was explained to me that homosexuals like to have sex with others of the same gender, I found the whole notion pointless and inconceivable, like concrete clothing or square wheels. Later, when I grew a bit older, homosexuality seemed to be associated with anuses and fetishes and raunchy pornography—an impression which, come to think of it, gay activism in the 1970s did as much as it could to reinforce. In any case, homosexuality was clearly about certain acts of sex, which I felt were of no interest to me. What I was in the dark about was something which in fact much or most of the world still misunderstands: homosexuality is not about what you may or may not do for sex, it is about whom you fall in love with. If I had imagined, then, that it was possible to love a man, as opposed to putting my penis here or there, perhaps things would have been different. On one point, all those years ago, my instinct was correct: without love, homosexual sex, like heterosexual sex, is at best an ephemera and at worst a lie. I felt no desire for sex, then, because I felt no capacity for love.

So I was not, mainly, lying to myself in my belief that homosexuality, as I understood it, was simply not relevant to my own condition. I was not lying when I blandly affirmed to myself or to Mary or to whomever that homosexuality had nothing to do with me. In fact, I was perfectly at ease talking about homosexuality as a social or psychological issue, if it came up in conversation. Why not? But of course to say this is not, yet, to touch the bottom. It was not merely naïveté or misconception which kept me in the dark and turned me upside-down. I was no fool: I knew by the age of fifteen or sixteen that male homosexuals worshipped the masculine eros, just as I did, and that there was more to sexuality than coarse sex. I was no passive drifter on my sea of perversion. No: I was hard at work, frantically, desperately denying.

But why? I did not regard homosexuality as immoral (that was for the God squad). So why the mad flight? I can only assume, trite as it is to say, that the cultural contempt for homosexuals which was still rife in that period (the 1970s and 1980s) permeated me as it did most other boys. A few gay boys and young men had the strength to be rebels, and a few others lacked the knack for blending in. But I—all I wanted was to be normal, which is really what any child or teenager wants. To be a homosexual was to be an oddball, always to be the one without a place at the table. Perhaps it was not so very peculiar, then, that I preferred being privately neurotic to being publicly scorned—a criminal in many states (until 2003!) and, until I was thirteen, still regarded by official psychiatry as mentally ill. Perhaps it was not so peculiar that I feared the exclusion from bourgeois life which all—left and right—agreed was the homosexual's fate; that I was loath to be a veritable symbol of decadence and immorality; that, above all, I shuddered at being transformed into an object of fear and disgust to good people like Paul's mother and father. The truth is, indeed, that the thought of homosexuality, for all my intellectual tolerance, viscerally disgusted me, because I had grown up with the assumption that homosexuality was disgusting, or in any event too nasty for open discussion. So I fought it with everything at my disposal. I turned the world upside-down to keep myself right side up.

It is inexpressibly heartening to see, today, a whole generation of young homosexuals—or anyway a big slice of a generation, enough to mark off today's group as different from any that has gone before—grow up wondrously aloof from the disgust I took for granted. They cannot imagine why they should be expected to hide, and often they do not hide (though often, still, they do). It is also gratifying to find, as I finally found, that today one may view one's homosexuality as a fact rather than as a secret, yet still be treated by most people with civility and generosity. For me the astonishing thing was to discover how possible it is to live as an open homosexual. When at last I stood on the threshold of coming out, I expected that what awaited me was a time of exhausting struggle and conflict and probably social rejection. I expected the world to turn and stare at me, as though I had vomited at a dinner party. Imagine my amazement at finding that, for most people, homosexuality is boring. And to see some of the homosexuals now in their teens and twenties is to behold people whose homosexuality is not particularly interesting even to themselves. It is now possible to meet many people, gay and straight alike, to whom homosexuality, as such, is unremarkable. That is the most gratifying thing of all.

I think that inversions of the kind I experienced are becoming rarer and will grow rarer still. I do not think, though, that inverts and their kin (desperate deniers, closet cases) will ever vanish, or even become all that unusual. It will never be easy to accept that to love as other people love, one must distinguish oneself from them. Even when homosexuality is viewed as ordinary, the homosexual is not ordinary— not quite. And amid those young people seemingly floating blithely apart from the upside-down world which imprisoned me, there are those like Michael G. A few years ago, he read something I wrote and sent me a letter. He admired my openness. But that was because he so disgusted himself:

> I am a coward. I have lots of excuses for myself—lingering doubts, a reluctance to give up on finding the right woman (even if, practically speaking, I have), fear of a "no turning back" decision, and the always handy Catholic shame/Jewish guilt. It's more than a little pathetic, in my late thirties, to be terrified of revealing any of this even to my closest friends (as if they'd all be shocked). ... For what you wrote and who you are, I am cheering for you, however quietly and in the safety and solitude of my apartment. But, in the end, I fear the ostracism.

I could say to him a hundred things. I could say that the ostracism is not remotely as oppressive as the dread of it; that lovelessness corrupts the soul, and cowardice the spirit, far more than homosexuality, or sexuality of whatever sort, corrupts anything; that when he has come to see himself as a coward he has already gone too far toward truth-telling to turn back; that in any case no one except probably his parents—a big "except," I grant him—much cares whether he is gay, and most people mainly want him to be happy. But there was really nothing I could say to him: just resoundingly, deafeningly, nothing. I was an invert (denying even to myself) whereas he was a closet case (comprehending but paralyzed), but our conditions were alike in one respect, and that is solitude: the certainty that no one, anywhere, could speak to our situation or penetrate our prison. Michael G. already knew all of the things I might have told him. He knew that he was corrupting himself by clinging to a deception, he knew that hesitation is more painful than action, he knew his friends would hardly be shocked. Above all, he knew what I, also, knew: that he was pathetic. But the fear and doubt were too strong, and his spirit quailed before them. Until the time comes—which, eventually, it must—no words could reach him. That is the last and most sadistic torment of his prison: the prisoner himself holds the key. "Go ahead, let yourself out!" taunts the warden. This prison is not only isolating; worse still, it is humiliating.

Many homosexuals believe it is demeaning to ask heterosexuals for compassion, but I do not think so. To be homosexual is not pitiable, but it is not easy. However, to be an invert or a closet case *is* pitiable, as the subject himself so acutely knows. People of compassion, then, will help homosexuals thrive, not strew obstacles in their path. This means, above all, allowing them to love and encouraging them to love. I doubt that many red-blooded heterosexuals can really imagine what the loveless imprisonment of an inversion or a closet is like, any more than the sighted can easily imagine what it is like to be blind. But if people understand that a gulag of the heart exists, and if they respond tenderly to homosexuals struggling to escape, then that by itself will be what Jews call a mitzvah and what Christians call a good deed. Please pray, then, that Michael G. has found, by now, the strength to love a man. For without a man's love—and there is no other love for him—what is he? What was I?

10

I KNOW how the story is supposed to end: happily ever after. Mainly, it does. But I could not grow up an invert, all the way from pre-adolescence through full (physical) manhood, without tying some knots in my personality which will never be undone. The inversion itself is mercifully just a memory, but like any childhood ailment, it left scars and neurotic kinks. They are manageable kinks, scars visible mostly to myself only, and they are not interesting enough to be worth describing here. Suffice it to say that love—whole, erotic, trusting, passionate love—still does not come as easily to me as it does to many people, and that the wholesome appreciation of physical beauty is still sometimes faintly but discernibly tinged with a discoloration of "envy," which really is self-hate. I write vaguely here, I know, but it is best not to finger one's scars. The point is merely to remind you that a total eclipse of the erotic personality does not come cheap. It can be ended but never entirely reversed. The best thing is to avoid it. That is why I hope that the denial of homosexuality comes to seem a very silly thing, and it is one reason I decided to publish this book. But there is another.

One cannot have lived differently. A fallacy of modernity is the belief that we, or our parents, build our personalities. Some parents I know act as though the slightest mistake or inadequacy on their part will tip their children's lives into a spiral of failure. In fact, life, as actually experienced, unfolds as a succession of givens, and our personality surrounds and shapes us from the start. If anyone can attest to that, it is the person who grew up ambushed and defeated at every turn by a nature he desperately sought to deny. So in the end—and in the beginning—one lives as one lives. I did as I did, no regrets. What else could I have done? But how I do ache, sometimes, over the theft of my youth. I would so have loved to flirt coltishly, to play teasing erotic games, to ask out a boy my own age and be rebuffed and try again and maybe win him. All of that is a blank for me. Love, like language, is best mastered young, and well into my thirties, I had a much younger man's knowledge of it. Sometimes I try to imagine life if I had been able to hope, at age fourteen, to kiss someone I adored, and maybe to be kissed back. Of course, many boys and girls wait quite a while for that first kiss, and when it comes it is often disappointing. Of course. Nonetheless, kissing shines in their imaginations from an early age, a daytime obsession and a nighttime lullaby: above all, it is the promise of a benediction to come. My inversion was a calm but leaden certainty that there would be no making love or loving for me, that all of my desire stretched outward toward—nothing. The inversion was a grotesque attempt to understand why it might be that for me, and me alone in the whole world, there was no one to kiss.

I recall a love affair that ended sadly. I was 36. He was a sweet and gentle man who left me. I missed him and felt bereft and abandoned and all the rest of it. But with the bereavement came the most curious note of satisfaction. I lost him, but before losing him I'd *had* him! In our kisses was an entire future. For a former eunuch, the loss of love is more sweet than bitter. I am the man who is grateful to fall down because he once believed he would never walk. I am still not a particularly good walker, but my clumsiness is itself a kind of victory. And as I write these words, I have been married for almost ten years. *Married.* The very word is a miracle to me. The young boy sitting on the piano bench structured his life, fought his personality, twisted and then untwisted himself around the certain knowledge that he could not love in a way which could lead to marriage; and so he grimly determined that he could not love at all. But he was wrong. He underestimated himself and he underestimated his countrymen even more. They and he have found a destination for his love. They and he have found, at last, a name for his soul. It

DENIAL

is not *monster* or *eunuch*. Nor indeed *homosexual*. It is: *husband*.

I try to get up every morning and be grateful. Most mornings, I succeed, though there are times when unfixed dents in the car or dishes in the sink make me forget. Mine may be the first and also last American generation to experience same-sex marriage as a source of profound gratitude and wonder, rather than as either an impossibility or an entitlement. I am grateful for that, too.

I have not, however, paid all my debts.

For twelve years, my deformed sexuality had a name, even if my soul did not, and the name was not *homosexual* or *invert* or even *freak*, but *Paul*. A junior-high-school crush is supposed to wear off quickly. It is supposed to be supplanted by the next crush and then by a real romance. For year after year, though, I wondered helplessly why I throbbed in Paul's presence, why the power of his arms and hands thrilled me. Moving away from home diminished my fixation but by no means extinguished it. The many other men I noticed gave me jolts of uncontrollable "envy," but no one, in all those years, could push Paul away. He was the sun around which my inversion revolved, and in that darkness, he was the only human figure. All the other objects of desire were glances, images, pictures; but he was a friend, which is maybe why I felt safe in his presence. In high school we spent hours together over algebra, gossiped together during lunch hour, and of course spent those blessed afternoons in the gym. I asked him all about his workouts, his muscles, every change in his blossoming body. Sometimes, pulling off a T-shirt, he would point to a new ridge or bulge, and I would nod sagely, hoping all the while that he could not hear my heart pounding. Later, in university, I would wait all term long to rush home for the winter or summer holiday to see—literally see, as in "behold"—Paul, and to admire how he had broadened his back or thickened his legs. I was careful not to touch him except "innocently." Sometimes, though, I would take the liberty of squeezing his arm and telling him how big and hard it was. He would demur and then—bless him!—find something encouraging to say about my scrawny body. When, ever so gingerly, I began experimenting with weights myself, making hardly any progress, he went out of his way to praise whatever little change he saw, as an older brother might have done.

I tried not to frighten either of us, especially myself, and I tried to disguise my obsession as best I could, but sometimes—maybe often, come to think of it—I would push too far, asking him one question too many about his abdominals or pestering him too insistently to flex an arm. On such occasions, he would rebuke me mildly for asking him to "show off," but never in our long acquaintance did he withdraw from me or deprive me of his intoxicating presence. Never, even, did he say an unkind word. When someone else noticed his physique, he would report the comment to me, knowing I would savor it. It was as though he sensed that I was imagining myself in his body, and he let me dress up in him. He was, in that way, sharing himself with me.

In retrospect, it seems pathetic, my desperate and unceasing effort to own and adore Paul, to see him, to brush against him, to imagine how much more muscular he might yet grow. It was not love but a kind of pre-erotic physical dependence, like a confined dog's dependence on its master for food. Yet to look back on it is also to be slightly charmed by the ingenuousness, and ingeniousness, of our "affair." I spoke earlier of the symbiosis between heterosexual vanity and homosexual lust, but that is a bit too simple, because, strange though it is to say, I was not conscious of my lust and he was not conscious of his vanity. It was precisely because we were both so naïve, and I was so confused, that we were able to use each other as we did, ministering to each other without knowing why or how. As long as I never told either of us how I felt about him, he could, in all innocence, let me admire him, enjoying it and understanding that somehow it was necessary for me.

The obsession with him faded and died soon after I finally acknowledged its nature. It just withered and blew away, like the rest of the inversion. When I became free to suppose that I was experiencing nothing more peculiar than ordinary young lust, and that I might love another and be loved in return, my vision caught up with my age and Paul shrank to human proportions. He became a memory. I was freed to forget him, and so, for the most part, I did. Sometimes when I went home I looked him up, and when I saw him with adult eyes I wondered how I could ever have been so entranced. He was only human, after all.

Of course, I never told him anything about the past. I never thanked him for putting up with my vampiric attentions. I never told him of my homosexuality, though the rest of the world knew. It all seemed too awkward, and I was afraid of what he might imagine me to have been up to during all those times together, and in any case it was all so long ago. And then one day, as life's tame middle stretched before me, I realized that I had never since felt for anyone the sort of frame-wracking passion which for so long I felt for him, and I remembered how I had used him and our friendship while lying to both of us, and I recalled especially how he had been compassionate and gentle and never unkind. It occurred to me that I owed him, those many years ago, a love letter. And now I have written one.

DENIAL

Afterword to the 2019 Edition

I wrote this book in 1996, when I was turning 36 years old. My period of inversion, constituting the whole first 25 years of my life, was already fading from memory. I had to work to reconstruct what was by then a long time ago. The book was an effort to do so—much as one jots down dreams which one knows one will soon forget.

At that point, I was beginning what would become the defining mission of the post-inversion portion of my life: the struggle for marriage equality. The first paragraph of the book is about marriage. It describes a moment in childhood when I realized I would never get married, although I had no idea why. My first conscious realization of my homosexuality, in other words, revolved not around sexuality, nor even around love, but around marriage. Children understand marriage long before they understand love or sex. For me, that I would never marry was not only the first realization but the worst. Had I been able to assume, or even imagine, as a young boy, that I might eventually marry someone I love, perhaps the whole inversion might never have happened.

In 1996, I believed I was writing a keepsake, a memento. In hindsight, I see that I was writing a manifesto. Although the word *marriage* appears only six times in the book (three of them in the first couple of pages), marriage is really what this book is about. Life without any hope of marriage is life without any destination for love, and therefore life without a soul. Looking back, it occurs to me that the second half of my life, which was preoccupied with marriage equality, was the antidote to the first half. This book is the hinge.

For seventeen years, *Denial* went unpublished. In the 1990s, before ebooks, I could find no takers for so short a book. Publishers liked it but did not see it as a commercial proposition. Truthfully, neither did I. Like all authors, I wanted to see my work in print, but inwardly, with the inversion only a decade behind me, I did not feel ready to put these raw emotions out there. Also, the people mentioned in the book were still very much around and part of my life, and the relationships were often unresolved, and I didn't feel quite ready to turn all of those people into characters, even though I changed everyone's name and disguised potentially identifying details. And so, after a handful of rejections, I pulled back *Denial* and put it in a drawer, which sometimes is the best place for a book.

By 2013, the world was a different place. I was married under District of Columbia law (although not under federal law), electronic publishing had made short ebooks a going proposition, and the events and people described here had receded into the past. By that point, I had come to see the book for what it really is, a *cri de coeur* for same-sex marriage, which I had come to understand was the key to soulful equality as well as legal equality. *Denial* was brought out by Atlantic Media and stayed in print until Atlantic dropped its ebook line in 2019. I am grateful to David Dalton and his Acorn Abbey imprint for picking up *Denial* and keeping it available, I hope, for many years to come. David makes a cameo in the book: he is the older gay man who gently affirms that what I feel for Paul might, just possibly, be love. He was among the first to read *Denial* in manuscript, and it finds a natural home in his wise and tender hands.

In the course of rereading it, now at a remove of 23 years, I find that it is no longer a memoir; it is a biography. By that I mean that I no longer know the person it describes. Whereas in 1996 I could with effort reconstruct my prison, in 2019 all that is left is a ruin: here a fragment of a wall, there a rusty shackle. Today my marriage has been federally recognized for four years and is no longer controversial, outside certain religious precincts. I live with my husband, Michael, in the suburbs of northern Virginia, where our life is the very picture of bourgeois normality. The neighborhood children and their parents regard us as a couple just like everyone else. I have come almost comically far from the monster I once thought myself to be. Only a few neurotic kinks remain to remind me of the first 25 years. I suppose I may in time lose even those. At this point, I would miss them.

Unfortunately, even in today's (comparatively) halcyon era, this book remains relevant, and not only for gay and lesbian people. The biggest surprise to me, when *Denial* was published, was how many heterosexual men (and a few women) told me it resonated with them. I thought: "Seriously? This is a book about a *homosexual* in denial about his *homosexuality*." But straights assured me that they, too, had imagined that they were monsters and no one else was like them and they would never fit in. To be honest, I still don't fully understand what might constitute a straight form of inversion, but I have come to accept, on the basis of many assurances, that such a thing must happen, and quite often. This is a book, then, for all people who are queer—gay queers and straight queers.

Today the professor is dead, the youthful version of me is a stranger, and much else has changed. For this edition, however, I have not made updates to reflect subsequent developments, nor have I reached outside the book's original temporal boundaries. I have made only light corrections and adjusted a few infelicities. I also added one anecdote which in 1996 I did not feel at liberty to include.

But I do feel there is one more story to tell.

At the time when I wrote *Denial*, I had been "out," which is to say openly homosexual, for years. Parents, family, friends, professional acquaintances, and readers of *The New Republic* (among other publications) knew I was gay. The whole world knew. Yet there was still one person I had not found the courage to tell. Perhaps he knew, perhaps he didn't, but somehow to have The Conversation with him would open me to ridicule or contempt or loathing which I still couldn't handle. He might assume that for all those years I had been nothing more than a predator. Or he might, by reacting badly, shatter my warm feelings for him. Such were my rationales, but, really, I'm not sure why I couldn't break that one final barrier. I suppose it was the last wall of my self-imprisonment. I am speaking of Paul, of course.

Not long after the book was written, on a visit to Phoenix, I connected with him and we had lunch together. It was one of those perfect crystalline days which bring people flocking to the desert in winter, and we were sitting at a table outside in the shade. At that point, I was still seeking a publisher for *Denial*, and I knew publication would spill all my secrets to

Paul, and so I had no choice but to bite the bullet and tell him. Reader, you will be shocked to learn that he wasn't very surprised. I asked if it had ever occurred to him, back when we were kids, that I might be gay and might have a crush on him, and he replied that he had been too busy with his own teenage problems to give it any thought. That made me chuckle, because, I said, I always had assumed his life was perfect (because he was perfect), and that I was the only one with problems. He asked what it had been like for me back then. I told him that if he was really interested, I had written a little memoir—and he was in it. He asked to read it. With trepidation, I gave it to him.

I heard back a day or two later. He said he had enjoyed reading the book. I asked how it all had seemed to him, what I got right or wrong, what other reflections he might have. All he said was that he had enjoyed reading it and thought it was interesting and well written. His bland, courteous reaction was the one response I was completely unprepared for. That's all? "Well," I thought, nonplussed, "at least I've told him, and I guess he doesn't care, and now I can move on."

I was even less prepared for what he said next. Why had I changed his name? I explained that I had changed all the names in the book, and changed or hidden identifying details, so as not to embarrass people. Also, I thought using real names and real identifiers would be a distraction; I wanted the figures in the book to be characters in their own right, separate from the outside world.

"Well," he said, "you can use my real name. I'd like if it you did."

His name was Warren.

—Fairfax County, Virginia, June 2019

www.ingramcontent.com/pod-product-compliance
Lightning Source LLC
Chambersburg PA
CBHW030057100526
44591CB00008B/176